Montana's Grandest: Historic Hotels and Resorts of the Treasure State

Sunny Side Hot Springs, Montana's Favorite Health Resort.

This 1910 postcard is from the mystery resort of Sunny Side Hot Springs apparently located near Alhambra Hot Springs.

MONTANA.   A DAUGHTER OF THE ROCKIES.

Greetings from MONTANA

Montana's Grandest:

Historic Hotels and Resorts
of the Treasure State

BY STAN COHEN

*To Clarence,
Best Wishes
Stan Cohen
8-8-04*

Pictorial Histories Publishing Company, Inc.
Missoula, Montana

LIBRARY OF CONGRESS
CONTROL NUMBER 2004092570

ISBN   1-57510-111-4

First Printing: June 2004

PRINTED IN KOREA
BY CORDA ENTERPRISES, INC.

COVER DESIGN: *Mike Egeler, Egeler Design*
TYPESETTING: *Leslie Maricelli*

Title page photo of the Broadwater Hotel, Helena.

PICTORIAL HISTORIES PUBLISHING COMPANY, INC.
713 South Third Street West, Missoula, Montana 59801
Phone: (406) 549-8488   Fax: (406) 728-9280
E-mail – phpc@montana.com
Website – pictorialhistoriespublishing.com

INTRODUCTION

When I first started my research on historic hotels and resorts in Montana a few years ago, I thought I might find a few dozen to write about. After doing extensive research at the State Archives, the Historic Preservation Office and traveling throughout the state, I found a myriad of locations, either full-blown restored buildings, those being restored, some buildings still standing but no longer in use as well as some sites long gone.

These structures can be found in every part of the state from the large cities to the rural areas. It has not been too many years ago that most every town of any size had one or more prominent buildings that served as hotels. Life-style and travel changes through the years doomed most of these hotels and resorts. It is interesting to note that all the early resorts in the state were located in areas where there was either mineral or hot springs activity. A few of these are still in business today: Gregson (Fairmont) Hot Springs; Chico Hot Springs; Boulder Hot Springs; Lost Trail Hot Springs; Symes Hot Springs; Quinn's Hot Springs; Jackson Hot Springs and Elkhorn Hot Springs.

The book is divided into two parts: Historic hotels and resorts that are operating today, such as: The Grand Union in Fort Benton; the hotels of Glacier National Park; The Izaak Walton Inn; The Northern in Billings and The Hotel Kalispell to name a few.

The second part of the book covers the grand and not so grand hotels and resorts that have either vanished from the landscape or are structurally remaining but not used for their original purpose.

Some current hotels and resorts have a long and interesting story while others were difficult to find much information. And some facts and dates were inconsistent in the literature. I have done the best I can to sort out the facts and be as accurate as possible.

Many of the existing sites are listed on the National Register of Historic Places and are duly noted. Others have been brutally altered and some are in different phases of preservation. Several are now on private property.

It would be nearly impossible to cover every existing or lost hotel or resort in the state but I have tried to pick what I think are the most important ones. Some cities had dozens of hotels in their colorful history. Great Falls had two magnificent hotel buildings which have been saved and have adapted their uses. Missoula had several dozen hotels in its history and surprisingly 10 structures are still standing in the downtown area. Helena may have had some of the most ornate buildings but, sadly, urban renewal brought down most of them.

These hotels and resorts are just one part of the fascinating history of Montana. So sit back and enjoy a trip into the past and when traveling around the state, be aware of these fine historic sites.

Stan Cohen

PHOTO SOURCES

TAYLOR COLLECTION–BILL & JAN TAYLOR, MISSOULA
MHS–MONTANA HISTORICAL SOCIETY ARCHIVES, HELENA
UM–UNIVERSITY OF MONTANA, K.ROSS TOOLE ARCHIVES, MISSOULA
HPO–HISTORIC PRESERVATION OFFICE, HELENA
OTHER PHOTOS ARE ACKNOWLEDGED TO THEIR SOURCE. PHOTOS NOT ACKNOWLEDGED
ARE FROM THE AUTHOR'S COLLECTION OR WERE PROVIDED BY THE INDIVIDUAL HOTELS/RESORTS.

ACKNOWLEDGMENTS

Many people helped in the production of this book. It could not have been done without their input. I would like to thank: The staff of the Montana Historical Society; Kate Hampton of the Montana State Historic Preservation Office; Philip Maechling of the Missoula Historic Preservation Office; Judy Ellinghausen of the High Plains Heritage Center, Great Falls; Ann Butterfield and staff of the Gallatin County Historical Society; Cas Sill and Andy Baxter of the Belton Chalet; Bob Keenan of the Bigfork Inn; Fran Brown, Alhambra Hot Springs; Barb Reiter, Boulder Hot Springs; The staff of the Butte Archives; Colin Davis, Chico Hot Springs; Patty Loraas, Elkhorn Hot Springs; Larry and Vivian Roland, Missoula; Michael Gordon, Butte; Jack Lepley, Fort Benton; Kenneth Robison, Great Falls; Bill and Jan Taylor, Missoula; The staff of the Western Heritage Center, Billings; Cheryl Gagnon of the Grand Union Hotel; The staff of the Crazy Mountain Museum, Big Timber; Larry Edwards of the Grand Hotel, Big Timber; Ron Weber of the Graves Hotel, Harlowton; Gerald Miller, Harlowton; The staff of Fairmont Hot Springs Resort; The staff of the Izaak Walton Inn; Inge Peterson, Jackson Hot Springs; Joann Schadewitz, Kalispell Grand Hotel; Bob Stephens, Kalispell; the Wilson Family, Granite Hot Springs; the Hanson Family, The Fort at Lolo Hot Springs; Paul Shea, West Yellowstone; Sandra Iverson, Melten Hotel; Vinola Squires, Beaverhead County Museum; Jerry Moran Hansen, Anaconda; Connie and Russ Schuevert, Reed Point; Rebecca Hazlitt, Alberton; Brian Sparks, Yellowstone Gateway Museum; Donna White and Dan Kaul, Murray Hotel; Bob Van Riper, Northern Hotel; Bipin Patel, Olive Hotel; Mary Wolf, Miles City; The staff of the Granite County Museum & Cultural Center; Sue and Jim Jenner, Broadway Hotel; Penny Clark, Carbon County Historical Society; Denise Moreth, Quinn's Hot Springs; The staff of the Sacajewea Hotel; Jane Waldie, The Old Hotel; Sherry Hagerman-Benton, Sanders County Historical Society; Barbara Behan, Missoula; Jack Demmons, Missoula; Gil and Joann Mangels, Polson; David Murray, Yogo Inn; John Humphrey, Lewistown; Nick Kern, Potosi Hot Springs Resort; Mark Campbell, Baker; Sue McLees, Superior; Chris Daly, Missoula; Janice Bauer, Forsyth; Pat Haas, Glendive; John Fryer, Livingston; George Gardner, Whitefish; Maria Craig, Bureau of Land Management and Michael Gallacher of the *Missoulian*. A special thanks to John Cohen for scanning, Leslie Maricelli for layout and Bob Jones for editing/proofreading.

The historic Taft Hotel was the first and last stop in western Montana, only five miles from Lookout Pass on U.S. Highway 10 West. The town of Taft, Mineral County, was built before 1900 and at one time had a population of 3,200. It's boom years were between 1906 and 1908 when it housed workers building the nearby Taft Tunnel. The great forest fire of 1910 destroyed the town except for the Taft Hotel. The original bar was once the longest in western Montana. The hotel was torn down when Interstate 90 was built through the area in the 1970s.

TABLE OF CONTENTS

*DENOTES SITES LISTED ON THE NATIONAL REGISTER OF HISTORIC PLACES

Montana's Grandest: Gone But Not Forgotten

Montana's Grandest: Historic Hotels and Resorts Still in Existence

THE MONTANA, ANACONDA, MONT.

THE RAVALLI, AT HAMILTON, MONT.

THE BOZEMAN HOTEL, BOZEMAN, MONT.

THE GRANDON HOTEL, HELENA, MONT.

THE HOTEL FLORENCE, MISSOULA, MONT.

Some Leading Hotels in Montana, "The Treasure State."

THE LEIGHTON HOTEL, MILES CITY, MONT.

THE BELTON CHALET

WEST GLACIER

THE BELTON CHALET
BOX 206
WEST GLACIER, MT 59936
1-888-235-8665
1-406-888-5000
WWW.BELTONCHALET.COM
30 GUEST ROOMS (NO TV OR TELEPHONES)
TWO COTTAGES
RESTAURANT AND TAPROOM

The Belton Chalet, Flathead County, is one of five historic rail-road hotels still operating in the state (Glacier Park and Many Glacier hotels, Gallatin Gateway Inn and the Izaak Walton Inn). The Great Northern Railway completed its right-of-way over Marias Pass and into the Flathead Valley in 1891. A stop was established at Milepost 1196 and designated Belton, just a short distance from present-day West Glacier. A boxcar was set off the tracks and with various modifications served as a station until 1910.

Upon completion of the railroad, development began in the area. News of the great slendor of this wilderness area soon spread around the country and the new little town of Belton began to cater to the summer visitors. A post office was established in 1900 and the town name was changed to West Glacier in 1949. The railroad, however, retained the name Belton Station.

In 1910, President William Howard Taft signed a bill authorizing the establishment of Glacier National Park.

In 1911, Louis W. Hill, who had succeeded his father, James J. Hill, as president of the Great Northern Railway, started a project of building a series of hotels, chalets and public services within the new national park. Hill was apparently influenced by the architecture of the European Alps and brought the idea of it to the Montana mountains. He wanted to provide comfortable accommodations for the tourists his

railroad brought to the area, but did not want these accommodations to be intrusive to the environment.

Within the next four years, the railroad had constructed a series of Swiss chalet-style buildings along a scenic route for a distance of 100 miles within the park. The chalets were constructed according to a standard plan designed by the Spokane architectural firm of Cutter and Malgren.

Two cottages to the east were added in 1911 and a large dormitory, now the lodge, was constructed to the south in 1913. The dormitory had 24 bedrooms and a large lobby (104'x35'). Each bedroom had hot and cold running water. Bathrooms were communal and located "down the hall." A trellis-covered, eight-foot-wide, stone-lined path linked the chalet

with Belton Station and the tracks of the railroad.

After Hill built his series of hotels and lodges, and acquired ownership of Lewis' Hotel on Lake McDonald within the park, business for the Belton Chalet, which was outside the park boundary, diminished and the buildings began to "run down." By 1925 the railroad wanted to divest itself of the buildings and for the next few years the chalet was either closed or leased to a private party. The construction of U.S. Highway 2 in front of the chalet in 1932 physically broke the link between the chalet and rail travel.

The era of train travel and elaborate tourist-related facilities changed in the 1930s with the advent of automobile travel, campgrounds and low-cost cabin courts. The railroad sold the buildings after World War Two and they had a steady decline of use. By 1997, when the current restoration began, the buildings had been modified to accommodate road improvements and changing uses over the years. They were becoming run down and unsafe. The verandas on the main chalet were restored to their original configuration.

Though modern facilities have been added to the guest rooms, the buildings retain the Arts and Crafts ambience of the early 1900s. The Restaurant and Tap Room contain original wainscoting and an outdoor grill was fabricated from the hotel's original hot water boiler.

There are many stories about the Chalet. One such story: "The chalet had a Swiss gardener named Hauser who came each summer for several years from Menominee, Wisconsin. Mr. Hauser was an excellent gardener and kept the grounds around the area beautifully trimmed. There was a hedge all along the wall by the railroad tracks and many varieties of trees planted on the well-kept lawns. One man stepped off the train and asked, 'Is this Glacier Park?' When Mr. Hauser replied that it was, the man said, 'Why, it's not as big as Manitou City Park in Spokane!' He had mistaken the grounds in front of the Belton Depot and chalet for the entire Glacier National Park!"

The present owners, Andy Baxter and Cas Sill are proud of the fact that their business was designated a National Historic Landmark in 2000.

The east end of the original hotel with a 1925 White bus and a good view of the trellis covering the path.

A 1914 view of the original hotel (right), the two cottages and 24-room lodge in the background. The trellis and path to the Belton Chalet to the left.

Interior of the honeymoon suite bedroom.

Interior of the lobby.

Exterior of the cottages.

Close-up view of the lobby fireplace.

View of the Clark Cottage porch.

Front entrance with owners, Cas and Andy.

BOULDER HOT SPRINGS

BOULDER

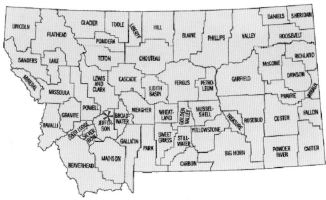

Nestled in the foothills of Montana's snow-peaked Elkhorn Mountains is Peace Valley, home of the Boulder Hot Springs, an historic landmark which once catered to presidents and wealthy ranchers. Boulder Hot Springs was claimed by a prospector in 1863, James E. Riley. In 1881, he enlarged the hotel at the springs, and the following year Riley began to construct a new hotel that would accommodate 50 people. In September of that same year, Riley died of small-pox. After Riley's death, Abel C. Quaintance and Cornelius Griswold bought the springs and the hotel was completed in 1883.

In 1890, C.K. Kerrick of Minneapolis secured a 10-year lease on the property. He supervised the construction of a large three-story addition to the old hotel structure with 52 guests rooms, renaming the hotel, Hotel May. At the time of the lease, the hot springs were two hours by rail from Helena and Butte. The Elkhorn line of the Northern Pacific completed that year brought rail service to a quarter mile from the springs. Kerrick disposed of his interest in the Boulder Hot Springs that same year to local businessmen. During this time period, the "Keeley Cure," a treatment for alcohol and drug addiction, was located at the springs.

The property changed hands several times, and in 1909, James A. Murray, a Butte millionaire miner and banker, purchased the springs. In 1910, the hotel under-went a thorough renovation and added a new wing at a cost of $200,000. Murray hired an interior decorator from New York City to redecorate the card room in a Chinese motif and do fancy fresco work in the huge lobby. Murray also hung the lobby's 12-foot ceiling with light globes of exclusive amber glass possibly made by Tiffany's of New York. Murray, who frequently visited California, was enamored of the architecture there, and added arches and fountains to the hot springs building plus having it stuccoed. The result was a huge building, resembling a Spanish mission. During the Murray years, there were many managers of the Springs, and it was often closed until someone would lease it. During the early 1930's gambling was legal, and it was also the time of the big bands, so Saturday night was a big night.

After the death of James A. Murray, his nephew, James E. Murray, later to become a United States

senator, became owner and he operated the hotel, with various managers, until 1940, when he sold to C.L. "Pappy" Smith. Pappy Smith changed the name to the Diamond S Ranchotel by which it was to be known for the next 35 years or so. The ranch was operated as a dude ranch, complete with trail rides and cook-outs. About 1960, Art and Beth Hulbert, relatives of Smith, came to work for him and instituted the tradition of Saturday night smorgasbords. These sumptuous meals, featuring baron of beef prepared by Walt Nettick, were enjoyed by an many as 400 or 500 people, with lines extending far out into the lobby.

Mr. and Mrs. Albert Lane purchased the Diamond S from Smith in 1960 and the ranch became a totally operating cattle ranch. They also operated the guest hotel, bar and dining room. A number of other owners were involved with the ranch/hotel over the years from 1965 through 1972, at which time Willard Mack and Robert Ryan from Billings purchased the property and subdivided the ranch. The next owner, Stewart Lewin, changed the name back to Boulder Hot Springs. Lewin attempted to make a success of the place for 11 years and was finally forced to close in 1989. In his years as owner, Lewin rebuilt the bathhouse and the walkway leading to the outdoor pool; opened one wing of rooms, put in a new kitchen and small restaurant and made other repairs. The property was returned to the former owners, Willard Mack and Robert Ryan.

In early 1990, the resort was purchased by a limited partnership including well-known psychologist, Anne Wilson Schaef, the author of numerous books. A great deal of time and money was spent on renovation and repairs and in the summer of 1991, the resort was reopened. The spa buildings, the small dining room and the east wing of the hotel (the 1910 addition) have been completely refurbished and are open to the public. The original 1891 portion of the hotel has retained the look of when it was refurbished in 1910 and there are plans to open this wing in the future.

The resort is located just off Highway 69, three miles south of Boulder in Jefferson County. Thirty-two springs flow from the hillside behind the hotel ranging in temperature from 125° to 180° F. The outdoor pool, behind the hotel is kept at 95° F and the men's and women's indoor pools average 104° F. There are 33 rooms in the 1910 addition and the resort's main function is to provide a quiet place for workshops, retreats and overnight guests. Breakfast is served every morning for guests and a buffet lunch is featured every Sunday.

The remains of the open air pool at the east end of the complex.

The resort when it was known as the Diamond "S" Ranchotel.

The present outdoor pool at the rear of the hotel was constructed in 1910 and reconstructed in 1974.

A 1910 view of the completed resort buildings. The area between the 1890 and 1910 addition is connected by the veranda producing an interior courtyard that at one time had a fountain.
MHS #957-397, ASAHEL CURTIS

A close-up view of the hotel complex. The building portion on the right, including the bell tower dates from construction in 1883 and 1890. The left building and imposing veranda, running the length of the two buildings, were built in 1910. The original appearance was altered to resemble a Spanish Colonial Revival style of architecture, by stuccoing the exterior walls and the veranda and building arched openings to resemble a Moorish style. This view is from the 1920s. MHS #940-283

An open-air plunge at the east end of the complex was built around 1915. It was Olympic-size and built of brick with tile walls and an enclosed locker space at the north end. At one time it was covered, but a heavy snow caved in the roof. The pool has not been used since a 1935 earthquake damaged the structure. MHS #940-285

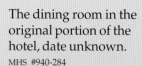
The dining room in the original portion of the hotel, date unknown.
MHS #940-284

Interior view of the main lobby in the 1890 addition showing the check-in desk area.

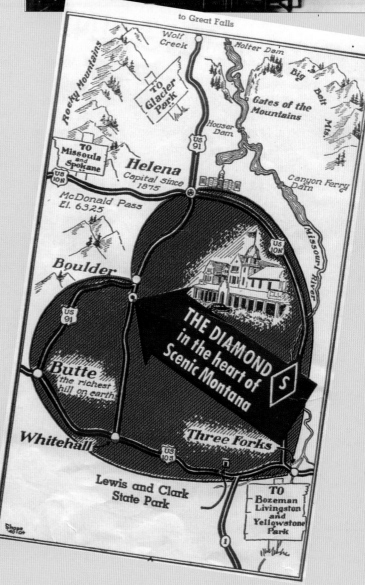

THE BROADWAY HOTEL

PHILIPSBURG

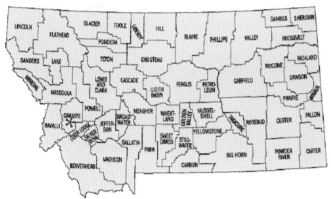

Montana's newest "old" hotel opened again in December 2003. It has been more than a quarter of a century since the last hotel closed in Philipsburg, Granite County. The "new" Broadway Hotel & Meeting Center is located on the upper floor of the 1890 J.K. Merrell Building on West Broadway in the historic mining town.

When it was built in 1890, the Merrill was one of the largest commercial buildings in the area. It had 12,000 square feet on two floors built into a side hill which permitted wagons to unload into the upper story from an alley in the rear. For several years after construction, the building was a general store including the company store for the Bi-Metallic Mines. Around 1900 the upstairs was converted into lodging space when mining activity in Philipsburg and Granite brought hundreds of workers to the area.

The building was used for a number of businesses through the years and saw the decline of the town when the mining played out. In the 1930s, when the building was a Penny's store, J.C. Penny actually served customers in the downstairs space. In recent years, there has been a great amount of new businesses and major restoration projects in town and Philipsburg has revived itself into a tourist destination area.

Sue and Jim Jenner have owned the building since the 1980s and in May 2003 restoration started. "Creating the Broadway has been a dream of ours for many years," said Jim Jenner, "We believe so much in the future of Philipsburg and feel that additional lodgings are sorely needed here in town."

They removed a number of walls and spaces that were added in the 1950s and later, refinished the 6,000 square feet of old growth fir floors and saved as much as they could of the original trim and window detail. The decor for the nine rooms reflects both the history of the area and the Jenners' years as documentary film producers. The Wrangler, Crosscut and Hard Rock rooms are dedicated to local ranching, logging and mining. The Sportsman's Club is a suite that includes its own poker table in a private sitting room. The Discovery Room looks out toward the local ski area. The Britannia Suite gets its name from Sue's birthplace in England and the Andes Suite, from their time living in Ecuador. The Route 66 Suite, from the PBS documentaries Jim created in the 1990s, and "Las Palomas" is the honeymoon suite complete with a two-person whirlpool tub. The room's decor is drawn from the three international award-winning films Jim has made on this family of birds (doves).

There is a large kitchen and coffee bar where guests eat a Continental breakfast. In the center of the building is a 900-square-foot guest lounge, which has a small stage, a fireplace and a large library and reading alcoves. The room can be used for large dinner parties or meetings. Guests can enter the hotel from the back without having to climb stairs to the second floor.

The fireplace corner.

The Discovery room.

The "Las Palomas," the honeymoon suite.

The library.

CAMAS HOT SPRINGS
SYMES HOT SPRINGS

HOT SPRINGS

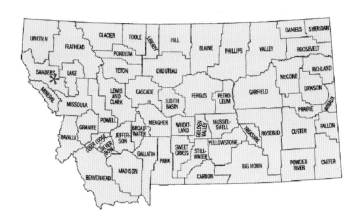

The town of Hot Springs in Sanders County has grown up around its thermal springs which have been used by Native Americans for perhaps thousands of years. Early settlers also frequented the numerous hot springs in the area.

The first commercial bathing facility in Camas Hot Springs was built by Ed Lemoreux in the early 1900s. It consisted of an eight-foot-square pool and two mud baths, one in a log cabin and one in a frame building. In 1910 the town of Hot Springs was incorporated and soon afterwards a large bathhouse was built containing seven rooms and eight tubs. The popularity of the area increased over the years and other bathhouses were built along with overnight accommodations.

In 1941, the springs ownership was turned over to the Flathead tribe and they started a major expansion of the facilities. In 1949, they opened their $400,000 Camas Bathhouse just northeast of the downtown area. The two floors were divided for men and women. Mud and mineral baths were provided along with an outdoor swimming pool. Massage therapy and steam baths were also available. The tribe also operated the "Corn Hole" foot baths where one could get treatment for disorders of the feet and lower extremities.

Camas Hot Springs became known nationally and even internationally for its facilities and its supposedly beneficial mineral water for the relief of arthritis, skin diseases, rheumatism, stomach ulcers, high blood pressure and many other ailments. Dozens of motels and tourist homes sprang up to service the guests. The hey-day for the business was in the 1940s, '50s and '60s but changing travel patterns and some economic blows to the area forced the tribe to shut down their major facility in the late 1970s.

Today two outdoor soaking pools are opened to the public, operated privately on a lease from the Flathead Tribe. One pool is a 10-by-15-foot concrete rectangle, four feet deep, the other is a smaller one, eight foot in diameter.

Camas Hot Springs' one remaining hotel is the historic Symes Hot Springs Hotel and Mineral Bath, located on Wall Street within the town's city limits. It was built in 1928 by Mr. and Mrs. Fred Symes. the building is constructed in a mission-style with pink-hued outer walls, looking somewhat like an

The historic Symes Hotel has retained its ambiance from its original construction.

old Spanish mission. It has been described as "one of Montana's last remaining grand resort hotels." The hotel has 22,000 square feet including 31 rooms, eight cabins and six apartments, a large lobby and sun room. Originally there were 20 large clawfoot tubs in private stalls where people could soak. today there is a two-tiered hot mineral pool with a waterfall in front of the hotel. Some of the large original tubs remain and there is a private soak and steam room that can be rented by the hour. There is a new day spa with a jetted hydrotherapy tub providing baths that stimulate, detoxify and give hydration and relaxation to the guest. The spa also offers Swedish massage, hot rock therapy, exfoliating scrubs and botanical wraps. Also available are private Watsu water massages, a form of massage developed in California.

The hotel is a "throw back" to an earlier time with no telephones or televisions in the guest rooms, and period furnishings, an open-air sun porch and an enclosed sunroom giving the guests a unique experience. There is also a restaurant, espresso bar, gift shop, hair salon and The Hot Springs Artist's Society sponsors live music, art exhibits and healing and educational workshops.

The Symes family sold the hotel in the mid-1990s to current owners Leslee and Dan Smith. They have added a 20- by 40-foot outdoor pool and now serve beer and wine in the restaurant.

MONTANA'S FAMOUS HEALTH RESORT

Symes HOTEL

MEDICAL SPRINGS

Medicinal Springs

HOT SPRINGS, MONTANA

Above: the Flathead tribe built a large bathing and health facility in Hot Springs in 1949. It closed about 30 years later and the building today sits abandoned.

The Hotel Florence was one of the larger hotels built in Hot Springs for the flourishing tourist trade of the 1940s, '50s and '60s.

CHICO HOT SPRINGS RESORT & DAY SPA

PRAY

CHICO HOT SPRINGS RESORT & DAY SPA
PRAY, MT 59065
1-406- 333-4933
CHICO@CHICOHOTSPRINGS.COM
WWW.CHICOHOTSPRINGS.COM
44 ROOMS IN MAIN LODGE, 16 ROOMS IN NEW LODGE,
HONEYMOON COTTAGE, FIVE BEDROOM LOG HOUSE,
TWO CHALETS
THREE RESTAURANTS
POOL & SPA
GROUP FACILITIES

One of Montana's most historic, well-known and popular resorts was named for a little Mexican man who was a great storyteller in the mining camp of Emigrant Gulch. His name was Chico and the gold mining area was located in Paradise Valley between Livingston and the future Yellowstone National Park. Six men from Virginia City, including Chico, had stopped at the camp in 1866 and told of the wonders they had seen in the Yellowstone country to the south. The miners then moved to a new camp near a hot springs and named it after the Mexican storyteller.

In 1883 two miners, Peter McDonald and Walter Matheson built some bathhouses at the springs and the resort was built up from that time. Three years later the Park Branch of the Northern Pacific Railroad was built through Paradise Valley. A bridge was built from the train stop at Emigrant Station to the bathing facilities. The popularity of the springs increased every year and in the 1890s local miner Bill Knowles and his wife, Percie Matheson, purchased the site. The two built a house near the springs and planned for a hotel and full-blown resort.

On June 20, 1900, the Chico Warm Springs Hotel in Park County was opened to the public with a great celebration. The two-story frame, clapboard hotel could hold 40 guests and had an enclosed plunge 44 feet in diameter and six feet deep. There were also private baths and baths for ladies with a designated stairway entrance direct from the hotel. Knowles also built a 24x50-foot dance pavilion.

On a hillside overlooking the resort, Knowles built a butcher shop, later converting it to a tasting room, including a bar and, later still, added a dance hall. Percie wouldn't allow liquor to be served at the resort itself. In the next few years, the swimming and bathing facilities doubled in size. A full-time physician was employed in 1902 to tend to the people coming to the springs for their therapeutic powers.

Bill Knowles died in April 1910 and the operation of expanding the resort was passed to his wife and 12-year-old son, Radbourne. Percie closed the saloon on the hill, and in 1912, hired Dr. George A. Townsend as the new permanent resident. The doctor was well-known and people came to Chico for his services. In 1916, a hospital wing was built on to the hotel. It could hold 24 patients and had a lab, operating room and six examination rooms. Dr. Townsend became known throughout the region and he once even performed surgery on a patient's brain (no mention of the outcome of the surgery). The doctor stayed on at the resort until retiring in 1925 but the resort continued to be known for its excellent health services.

By the late 1920s and into the Depression years, the business waned and at times most of the hotel was closed. Percie's physical and mental strength began to go and she eventually was taken to the Warm Springs State Hospital. The son and his wife struggled to keep the resort and hospital open but finally had to tear down the hospital due to its expense.

Radbourne Knowles died in 1943 and his wife sold the entire resort in 1948 to Oneita Behnke (later remarried and called Nita Broderick). She reopened the saloon, introduced gambling and changed the name to Chico Ranch. With her husband, they operated the resort as more of a dude ranch with horses, rodeos and a western living style.

In 1957, a strong wind caused the collapse of the plunge roof with more than 70 swimmers in the pool. Luckily, only two people were slightly injured. The pool was left uncovered, as it is today. For the next few years, there were several owners as the resort gradually fell into disrepair. One owner promoted the resort for religious camps and retreats.

A group from Cleveland bought the resort in 1973, and in 1976, the current owners, Mike and Eve Art bought the other owners out. With alot of hard work and many lean years, they have built their business into one of the best-known resorts and one of the finest restaurants in the state. The main hotel has been brought back to its antique heritage and has 44 guest rooms. The lobby is filled with historic memorabilia with no telephones or television. A new 16-room log lodge has been built west of the main lodge. There is also a honeymoon cottage, a small motel and a five-bedroom log house. There are also two chalets on the hill behind the lodge. Guests have a choice of three restaurants: the Chico Inn, the House of Ribs and the Poolside Grille.

The new lodge.

The outdoor swimming pool.

Chico Hot Springs and the Hospital in the spring of 1918. MHS #PAC 92-60

The three-story kitchen wing, added in 1919, brought Chico to its maximum capacity. GALLATIN
COUNTY HISTORICAL SOCIETY

A July 1919 view of the big new swimming pool showing Chico employees.
GALLATIN COUNTY HISTORICAL SOCIETY

View of the lobby in the 1930s.
GALLATIN COUNTY HISTORICAL SOCIETY

A 1939 view of the dining room.
GALLATIN COUNTY HISTORICAL SOCIETY

ELKHORN HOT SPRINGS

POLARIS

ELKHORN HOT SPRINGS RESORT
PO BOX 460514
POLARIS, MT 59746
1-406-834-3434
1-800-722-8978
INFO@ELKHORNHOTSPRINGS.COM
WWW.ELKHORNHOTSPRINGS.COM
11 CABIN RENTALS, 10 ROOMS
TWO OUTDOOR POOL
RESTAURANT AND BAR

Nestled in the Pioneer Mountains in Southwest Montana is Elkhorn Hot Springs in Beaverhead County It is a fairly remote resort, which enhances its charm. It is located on Forest Service Road 484 (Pioneer Mountain Scenic Byway) off Montana Highway 43 which cuts through the Big Hole Valley. Maverick Mountain Ski Area is four miles from the resort.

A 20x40-foot plunge had been built years ago but had fallen into disrepair. The land had come under ownership of the new U.S. Forest Service in 1905, but that year a man named Samuel Engelsjard filed water rights on the springs and built some cabins and a horse stable.

Jack Johnson Brown came to Montana from Idaho Falls, Idaho, and worked for the Edward & Olson Sheep Company near Armstead in 1920. He built a lodge at the springs in 1921 and in the 1920s and '30s, 11 cabins were built in the area. A series of owners ran the resort for six decades with little upgrade except for a poolhouse rebuilt in the 1940s.

In 1980, Bernal Kahrs bought the resort which was in a deplorable state. Through the years the resort was brought back to life and today the present owners, Orville and Patty Lovaas have a thriving business that is open all year. A redwood deck around the outdoor pool was added in 1992.

There are two outdoor pools and an indoor wet-sauna. The water flowing into the pools is all natural and gravity fed. It is high in mineral content and has no sulfur. Temperatures range from 95 to 100 degrees F for the outdoor pools and 102 to 106 degrees F for the indoor wet-sauna. Only one of the 11 cabins has indoor plumbing, all have been upgraded with electricity. They have purposely been left much like they were when built. The lodge is rustic and cozy and serves food and drink.

Besides the bathing facilities, the resort offers mountain biking and horse trail rides in the summer and cross-country skiing and snowmobiling in the winter. There are ghost towns and the Crystal Park Recreational Area close by and many other outdoor activities in the area.

The old lodge has 10 rooms on the second floor and a restaurant and bar on the first floor.

The 11 cabins are scattered throughout the property. They have wood stoves or fireplaces but no running water or indoor bathrooms.

The outdoor pools today. The larger one is kept at 95° F, the smaller one at 98° F.

FAIRMONT HOT SPRINGS RESORT

FAIRMONT

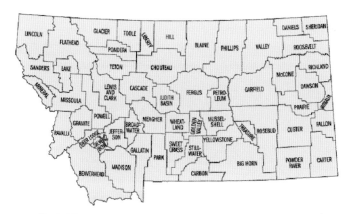

Two large hot springs occurrences are in the upper Deer Lodge Valley. One, Gregson, (Fairmont Hot Springs) in Silver Bow County is one of Montana's largest and prestigious resorts, the other is now and has been for some time, the site of the Warm Springs State Hospital.

Native American tribes such as the Flathead, Nez Perce and Shoshone set up their tepees at the Gregson site and used the hot springs long before white man knew about them. The Native Americans called the 12 hot pools, "Medicine Waters."

A man named Hulbert had squatted at the pools and in 1869, George and Eli Gregson purchased the property for $60. They also took up a claim to the 320 acres surrounding the springs. They initially went into the dairy business but later turned their attention to the 12 pools of hot mineral water.

A two-story hotel that could accommodate 50 to 60 guests was built along with a 30-foot by 48-foot plunge bath and five large bathing rooms. A barroom and separate sleeping apartments were built away from the hotel. A covered flume was used to bring hot and cold water to the bath houses. The cold water was drawn from a pure, cold stream flowing about 700 yards south of the hotel. There were 12 springs within an area bounded by a circle 50 yards in diameter. They ranged from 152 degrees to 161 degrees and by adding salt and pepper to the hot spring water a savory soup could be made which patrons hoped would cure various ailments.

Cures were advertised for rheumatism, neuralgia, catarrh, kidney diseases, arthritis and kindred diseases. Even what was called nervous prostration was supposedly cured by the medicinal waters. Butte was only 15 miles away and coaches ran daily back and forth. A railroad was constructed within one-half mile of the resort. Besides the hot springs, patrons could partake of hunting and fishing in the area or just relaxing from the noise, heat

and dust of Butte, Anaconda and other cities.

In 1890, the resort was leased to Miles French and in 1892, a townsite was plotted and 45-foot by 125-foot lots were laid out for sale. In 1901 the resort was sold to Con Hays and James Breen. Many clubs and organizations held parties and picnics at the resort and on Aug. 12, 1912, the Butte Miners held their annual picnic for 14,000 people. A brawl broke out between the Butte Miners and the Anaconda Smeltermen. Two men died in the melee. At the inquest, the judge could not determine what really occurred so no one was prosecuted.

As happened to many other hotels and resorts in the state, the dance hall and some adjoining buildings caught fire on Dec. 23, 1914. Nine days later, the plunge and other buildings also caught fire. Faulty wiring was apparently to blame. The Montana Hot Springs Corporation had owned the resort since 1906.

George Forsythe purchased the resort in 1916 and spent years upgrading and remodeling. According to a July 5, 1926, article in the *Butte Miner*, Forsythe built the largest carousel in the state and a new outdoor pool, the largest in the country. It also had a 125-foot "T" rail water toboggan. A new 18-hole golf course designed by Ted Barker, Montana's premier golfer, was constructed.

In either 1944 or 1945, Treasure States Industries took over the resort. In the succeeding years the resort deteriorated until it closed in August 1971, ending over a 100-year history. The resort was closed but would soon get a second life.

Federal funds were available to build a new resort including a large hotel, indoor and outdoor pools, an 18-hole golf course, tennis courts, restaurant and lounge. The resort would tie in with the area's hunting, fishing, horseback riding, skiing and snowmobiling. In early 1972, Lloyd Wilder of Fairmont Hot Springs in British Columbia, became the prime owner of Gregson Hot Springs. Reber Contractors of Helena was the prime contractor for the new resort and removed the remaining old buildings. Architect Ken Knight of Great Falls, designed the main building to be a cross of structures with an 80-foot by 120-foot indoor pool (on the site of the old outdoor pool) and a larger outdoor pool with a large slide.

Hotel rooms were in the south and west wings, the lobby and shops in the center, and dining rooms and convention center to the north. The lounge was located on the second level which connects to the second floor via an enclosed bubble walkway. At no time would one need to leave the complex to enter another area.

Wilder sold the resort, now named Fairmont Hot Springs, to Leroy Mays in 1981. In 1987, the resort was taken over by two financial institutions and in 1990, Wilder repurchased the resort to continue with his vision of providing complete resort services. Lloyd Wilder died in 1995 but the resort continues to be owned by his heirs.

The pond fed by the natural hot springs does not freeze in winter and is home to area ducks and geese. During the summer, the fountain adds to the lovely grounds of the resort.

The rider enjoys the descent down the 350-foot long, five-story waterslide. The slide is fed with the warm waters of the hot springs pools.

The lobby.

Outdoor pools and slide.

The year-round duck pond and surrounding countryside.

Suite interior.

Interior of Whiskey Joe's bar.

The Pintlar meeting room.

Ad from the
semi-weekly
Butte Miner,
Jan. 5, 1887.

A pre-1900 view of the
hotel at Gregson Hot
Springs. MHS #PAC 97-32.1

Front of the Gregson
Hot Springs Hotel. The
enclosed Natatorium
was 200' by 64'.

Dining room.

Main Dining Room,
Gregson Hot Springs, Mont.

1900 ad.

A postcard from 1917. The back side has the following: "What Dr. Starz, Ph.G., says of the water: 'Above water belongs in the class of alkaline waters and should give excellent results in catarrhal conditions of mucous membranes of the stomach and intestines; also in rheumatism and gouty conditions. It also possesses tonic properties.'"

Article from the *Butte Miner*, July 5, 1926

Gregson Springs
* * * *
Long Voted as Recreation Spot for Butte Folk.

A necessary adjunct to any city is a "playground."

Gregson Springs has long been noted as the recreation spot for Butte folk. Its beautiful surroundings and its hot springs, together with the excellent hotel and cafe service and its equipment for providing the best of "good times" for the urban dweller in search of relaxation, has made it not only a favorite gathering place for Butte people, but also famous throughout the entire state of Montana.

If, in the past, Gregson Springs has been made attractive to pleasure seekers, the coming Gregson is to be doubly attractive. Under the direction of Mr. George Forsythe, the best of Butte resorts is being remodeled into a playground for grownups as well as youngsters, which will not have a peer in the entire northwest. Hosts of workmen have been busy all the past month or two in installing additional "attractions" and adding to the already beautiful grounds.

For the big folk Mr. Forsythe has eration the largest carousal in the state and one of the biggest in the world is ready to provide its quota of thrills. The new outdoor pool, the largest in the country, has a special compartment where youngsters can paddle to their hearts' content without danger of getting in "over their head." A playground, modeled after the best of the kind in the civic centers in America, will provide any number of hours of fun for the children—children of all ages, too!

For the big folk Mr. Forsythe has opened the biggest outdoor pool in the country—fed by the famous warm springs and provided with a new thrill for Butte folk in the monster 125-foot "T" rail water toboggan. If you really want to get a kick out of pool bathing this toboggan will convince you there are some things you have not yet sampled. It has proven the most popular of all aquatic stunts wherever it has been installed, and Mr. Forsythe foresees a tremendous popularity for it here.

Ted Barker, Montana's premier golfer, has laid out what will be the most beautiful and sportiest course in the state. Eighteen holes, so arranged as to provide the golf fan with opportunity to try out every stroke in his bag and yet not too difficult to prove a burden on the average duffer, start and end at a new clubhouse provided with everything except the ancient nineteenth hole—gone but not forgotten! In the big pool room in the hotel the Springs management has provided lockers at a nominal rental, and a plunge may follow the round of the links for those so inclined. Queer little feature of this course which is bound to prove a blessing is this. At three of the tees out on the course are bubbling springs of clear, cold water. This course, half way between Butte and Anaconda, is bound to be immensely popular.

All in all, this new Gregson Springs is quite a place. It would have to be one mighty hard-boiled patron who couldn't find there almost anything he wants in the way of very real enjoyment.

FAIRWEATHER INN AND NEVADA CITY HOTEL AND CABINS

VIRGINIA CITY / NEVADA CITY

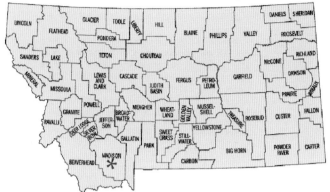

HISTORIC EXPERIENCE COMPANY
Box 57
VIRGINIA CITY, MT 59755
1-406-843-5377
1-800-829-2969
HOTEL ROOMS IN FAIRWEATHER INN
AND NEVADA CITY HOTEL
CABIN RENTALS IN NEVADA CITY

The town of Virginia City in Madison County is the result of the discovery of gold along a stream in Alder Gulch on May 26, 1863. Miners descended on the site in droves and on June 16, the Varina Town Company plotted the town. Some of the miners wanted to name the town Varina after the president of the Confederate States of America, Jefferson Davis' wife, Varina. Other miners were staunch Unionists and when it came time to file the official documents, the newly elected miner's court judge, Dr. G.G. Bissell, submitted the name Virginia instead.

Most of the population of Montana in the mid 1860s was now concentrated in the Alder Gulch area and Virginia City had an estimated population in 1864 of 5,000. The town became the second territorial capital in December 1864, a title it held until 1875 when the capital moved to Helena. Virginia City, Nevada City and Bannack became famous in 1863-64 with the formation of the Montana Vigilantes who hanged two dozen suspected outlaws.

After the railroad reached Butte from the south, bypassing Virginia City, the town went into decline. In the 1890s, huge gold dredges worked the Alder Gulch area. With the town on the brink of total abandonment in the 1940s, Charles and Sue Bovey of Great Falls began to buy up the buildings in town, beginning one of the first large-scale preservation efforts in the West. The town was designated a National Historic Landmark in 1961, listed on the National Register of Historic Places in 1976 and was purchased (the Bovey properties) by the State of Montana in 1997, along with Nevada City.

The present Fairweather Inn is an example of using an old building with many modifications. The oldest part of the building dates to 1863 as a one-story restaurant with a false front. A storefront was built in the 1880s with large plate glass windows and in 1896, it was turned into the Anaconda Hotel. In 1935, the Humphrey Gold Corporation, which operated dredges in Alder Gulch, bought the old hotel building and built a dormitory on the east side for its workers. After 1940, the building was abandoned until Charles Bovey bought it in 1946.

He added a second story, a new facade that duplicated the Goodrich House, an old hotel in Bannack, and added indoor plumbing. An old dredge ladder was put on the building for use as a fire escape. Bovey named the hotel after William Fairweather, the discoverer of gold in Alder Gulch.

Today the hotel caters to guests from around the world. It offers five rooms with tub-equipped bathrooms and one double bedroom on the second floor. The remaining main floor and upstairs rooms have shared bathroom and shower facilities. Each room has a sink.

NEVADA CITY HOTEL AND CABINS

Nevada City, one and one-half miles west of Virginia City, was also an old mining town in Alder Gulch. The Boveys bought this town along with Virginia City and brought in quite a few old buildings for display. The Nevada City Hotel was once an active stage station and offers western-style rooms with private bathrooms. Two special rooms are located on the second floor. Each is decorated with polished burlwood bedsteads, marble topped beds and high-back chairs.

The Nevada City Cabins are authentic old miners' cabins, refurbished with private bathrooms.

The Nevada City Hotel on Highway 287. LARRY ROLAND PHOTO

Rear view of the Nevada City Hotel showing the two-story outhouse. LARRY ROLAND PHOTO

The Fairweather Inn on Wallace Street in Virginia City. LARRY ROLAND PHOTO

A 1952 view of the Fairweather Inn lobby.

The Fairweather Inn in the 1960s.
GALLATIN COUNTY HISTORICAL SOCIETY
P4610, SCHLECHTEN PHOTO

Finlen Hotel and Motor Inn

FINLEN HOTEL AND MOTOR INN
100 EAST BROADWAY STREET
BUTTE, MT 59701
1-406-723-5461
1-800-729-5461
40 FULL-TIME APARTMENTS
2ND AND 3RD FLOOR HOTEL ROOMS
32 MOTEL UNITS
CAVALIER LOUNGE
GROUP FACILITIES

At one time Butte was the largest and most important city in Montana. But like other mining centers in the west, its fortunes were tied to the cyclic nature of metal prices.

Miles Finlen had worked in the great Comstock Lode in Nevada with future Butte copper king, Marcus Daly. Finlen was considered a "wild Irishman" who was tried for murder in Nevada but was acquitted. He came to Butte and did very well in mining ventures and bought the McDermott Hotel, which sat on the site of the present hotel.

He changed the name to The Finlen Hotel but it never made any money until his son, Jim, inherited the business after Miles died in 1911. Jim revitalized the business and ran it at a profit for the next 11 years.

The economy and metal prices were up and down through the years but by 1922 they had stabilized. Jim Finlen decided to build a grand hotel in Butte modeled after the Hotel Astor in New York City. Opened on Jan. 1, 1924, it was an elegant structure in uptown Butte and was originally supposed to have two towers. The first tower was completed in grand style including a mansard roof and copper sheathing. Economic conditions and the stock market crash of 1929 stopped construction of the second tower, however.

Even during the Depression years and the war years, the hotel was the social center of Butte. Guests have included three regiments of federal troops billeted in the hotel in 1920 during one of Butte's many labor strifes. Charles Lindbergh stayed at the hotel on his famous 80 city tour of the country after his famous 1927 flight to France. Three presidents, Richard Nixon, John F. Kennedy and Harry Truman have stayed at the hotel along with many other dignitaries through the years.

In 1979 Frank Taras took over the hotel and has spent years remodeling the structure including the beautiful lobby area. Today the building has 40 full-time rented apartments, with the second and third floors still rented out as hotel rooms. Adjacent to the main building is a 32-room motel. The Cavalier Lounge still operates in the main hotel building.

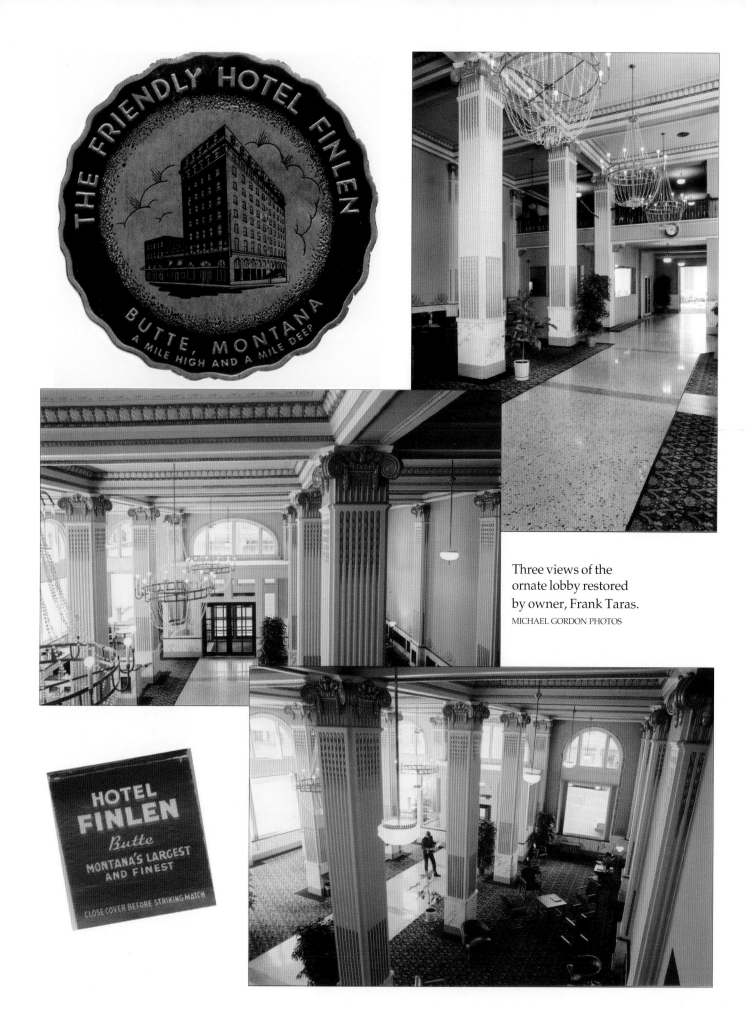

Three views of the ornate lobby restored by owner, Frank Taras.
MICHAEL GORDON PHOTOS

THE FINLEN HOTEL BY NIGHT. BUTTE. MONT.

A 1913 view of the Finlen Hotel, originally known as the McDermott Hotel, built in 1886. Miles Finlen purchased the hotel in 1899 and renamed it. The building was demolished in 1924 to make room for the current hotel.

1927 letterhead.

FINLEN HOTEL ARCHIVES

The Mission dining room as it looked in this 1914 view.

Dinner party in the ornate
dining room. Date unknown.
FINLEN HOTEL ARCHIVES

The Finlen Hotel was the site
for the Cold War Ground
Observer Corps in the 1950s.
This was a nationwide civil
defense organization to
watch for potential enemy
aircraft. FINLEN HOTEL ARCHIVES

Below right: the local
Butte Chevrolet dealer
showed the new line of
1950 trucks in the lobby
of the hotel. FINLEN HOTEL
ARCHIVES

1909 letterhead.

FORT PECK HOTEL

FORT PECK

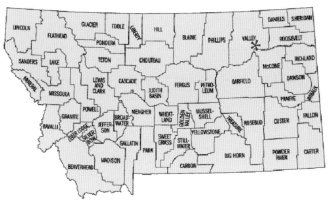

FORT PECK HOTEL, RESTAURANT & LOUNGE
BOX 168
FORT PECK, MT 59223
1-406-526-3266
1-800-560-4931
35 ROOMS
RESTAURANT AND LOUNGE
GROUP FACILITIES

One of the first and largest construction projects of President Roosevelt's New Deal Program, the Works Progress Administration, was the Fort Peck Dam on the Missouri River in Valley County, northeastern Montana. The dam's statistics are impressive. It is the largest earth-filled dam in the world at 21,000 feet long, 4,900 feet wide at its base and 250 feet high. The reservoir behind the dam has a surface area of 249,000 acres, is 134 miles long with a maximum depth of 220 feet and a shoreline of 1,600 miles.

To build this massive structure, 50,000 people lived and worked in the area at the height of construction in the mid 1930s. The Swiss chalet-style hotel was built in 1934 to house U.S. Army Corps of Engineers officers and employees. It has two stories with a hip roof and is rectangular in shape (184 feet by 45 feet) with a full-length front porch (10 feet wide) and a rear dining room (22 feet by 62

feet). It also has a shed roof dormer for third floor rooms along the central half of the south side.

Originally the building had a one-story dormitory wing at each end, one for men and one for

women. These buildings were removed in the 1950s. Interior alterations include new wood paneling for the wainscot along the stairs in the 1950s, a new heating system and insulation in 1978 and a bar in the lobby in 1980.

Today the hotel offers 35 rooms with two beds each; 11 rooms share two common full baths and shower rooms; 24 have individual baths, some with the original clawfoot bathtubs. The restaurant and lounge are inside the hotel.

The Fort Peck Hotel in the late 1930s and as it looks today.

GALLATIN GATEWAY INN

GALLATIN GATEWAY

GALLATIN GATEWAY INN
HIGHWAY 191, BOX 376
GALLATIN GATEWAY, MT 59730
1-406-763-4672
1-800-676-3522
GATEWAYINN@GALLATINGATEWAYINN.COM
33 ROOMS
RESTAURANT AND LOUNGE
GROUP FACILITIES

The Chicago, Milwaukee and St. Paul Railway had conquered the rugged mountains of western Montana and Idaho on its way to the Pacific Coast in the early 1900s. Soon part of the route was electrified and a spur line was built within 75 miles of the west entrance to Yellowstone National Park.

The company decided to build the first railroad hotel outside a national park, at the head of the Gallatin Valley and the end of the spur. The small town of Salesville (now Gallatin Gateway) in Gallatin County , 12 miles from southwest of Bozeman on Highway 85 was chosen.

On Feb. 18, 1927, ground was broken and with as many as 500 men working, the 42,000 square-foot Spanish-style building was completed in an astonishing four months. The hotel is a stately two-story structure with pale-yellow outside walls topped by a high peaked roof covered in red tiles. A marquee braced by four massive chains protects the entrance to the lobby. A broad semicircular driveway passes 100-foot pine trees placed in a large, well-groomed front lawn.

The elegant interior has a tall, glassed arch with a massive lobby "great hall"

and chandeliers like wagon wheels hanging from the high-curved ceilings. The front desk resembles an old-fashioned railroad ticket window. The spacious dining room seats 72 and the original 33 rooms offer the flexibility of single, double or two-room suites. Adjacent to the check-in area is a spacious lounge that once served as the baggage room. The original railroad clock in the lobby continues to keep accurate time and the original craftsmanship in the Polynesian mahogany woodwork, the decoratively carved beams and high-arched windows reflect a bygone time of luxury railroad travel.

The opening day ceremony on June 27, 1927, dominated Montana newspaper headlines–even Lindbergh's historic flight was overshadowed. VIPs included the governor, executives of the railroad, government representatives and Native Ameri-

BOB MURRAY PHOTO, BOZEMAN

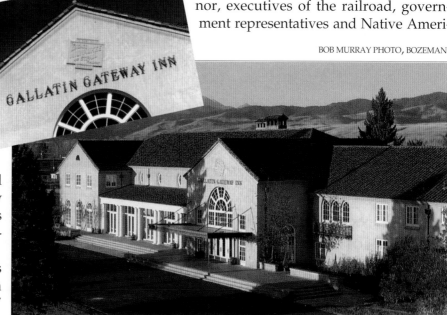

cans. The *Bozeman Daily Chronicle* claimed 20,000 visitors that day. The hotel was touted as one of the most luxurious and sophisticated of its day, from its advanced fire protection systems to the telephones in each room. The kitchen was so well stocked with a large array of electric marvels that women guests were enthusiastically encouraged to take tours. In 1940, the railroad made a full length film entitled, *Gallatin Gateway Honeymoons*, to promote their hotel.

Over 20,000 guests a season stayed at the hotel for the next several decades but by the early 1950s travel patterns, especially with the railroads, changed and the hotel was sold in 1951. A succession of owners tried to keep the hotel open but the business and the building gradually deteriorated. The first floor became a raucous saloon and eventually the guest rooms were converted into unappealing cold-water flats. Fortunately, the building was rarely modified so when it was sold again in 1986 and brought back to its former glory, it was mainly a matter of painting, repairing and general sprucing up. In 2002, POW Inc. from California purchased the property.

Today a guest can play croquet, sit in the hot tub or take a swim, have a great dinner and attend sessions of a fly fishing school or just enjoy the atmosphere of a beautifully restored hotel.

GALLATIN GATEWAY

into YELLOWSTONE PARK

The Historic-Scenic Route

GALLATIN GATEWAY to YELLOWSTONE NATIONAL PARK C. M ST P. & P. RR.

CHICAGO MILWAUKEE ST. PAUL AND PACIFIC

Through FAMOUS GALLATIN CANYON

A 1928 railroad brochure.
TAYLOR COLLECTION

Modern view of the restored lobby.
BOB MURRAY PHOTO, BOZEMAN

A 1927 promotional post card for the new Inn.

The
Chicago, Milwaukee and St. Paul
Railway

announces the opening of its new

Gallatin Gateway Inn

at

Gallatin Gateway, Montana

to be operated in connection with

its new service to

Yellowstone National Park

The honor of your company is
requested at the opening reception
and dance to be given

Friday Evening, June 17, 1927

from eight to twelve

C M & St. P. Ry Co's Inn.
GALLATIN GATEWAY, Mont.

The Inn is tastefully designed with stucco exterior, tile roof
and plaster inside, all planned to be in keeping with the surroundings.
It is located so as to have a commending view of the surrounding mountains.

The Inn has 26 bedrooms, 11 with private bath, 10 with com-
municating bath and 5 without bath.   There are 12 private dressing rooms
with lavatories and showers. There are toilet facilities on both the first
and second floors.

The Inn is electrically lighted and steam heated.

The dining room is artfully designed and will seat 160 at one
time.

The kitchen is of modern design and includes a refrigeration
plant, electric broilers, dish washer, etc.

Telegraph office and telephone booths; News, Cigar and Curio
stands and Manager's office are located near the foyer on the first floor.

Small bingalows are provided in proximity to the inn for
housing help, built to harmonize with the surroundings.

The approximate gross floor areas are as follows;

Basement	3,000 sq. ft.	
First floor	15,540 " "	
Second "	8,650 " "	
Total	27,190 " "	
Dining Room	2,652 " "	
Lounge	2,660 " "	(Has large open fire place)
Foyer	1,972 " "	
Baggage and parcel room	1,530 " "	
Kitchen	819 " "	
Veranda	840 " "	
Lobby	510 " "	
Women's rest room	240 " "	

Office of Chief Engineer
Chicago, Ill., Mar. 1, 1927
FDY

Specifications of the Inn have changed somewhat since this list was compiled in March 1927.

2414. Gallatin Gateway Inn, Gallatin Gateway
Entrance to Yellowstone National Park.

Views of the completed Inn in 1927.
TAYLOR COLLECTION

In the 1930s the railroad used limosines to transport tourists to the west entrance of Yellowstone National Park. TAYLOR COLLECTION

GALLATIN GATEWAY INN

Top: The railroad unloaded passengers on the back side/west entrance of the Inn. This photo is from July 1936.
Middle: The Inn provided various recreational opportunities for their guests. TAYLOR COLLECTION

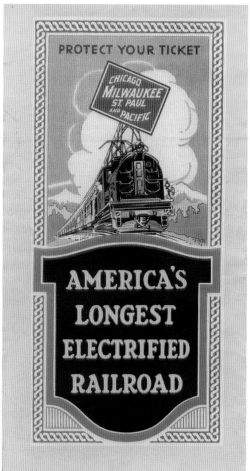

PROTECT YOUR TICKET

CHICAGO MILWAUKEE ST. PAUL AND PACIFIC

AMERICA'S LONGEST ELECTRIFIED RAILROAD

The Inn provided a relaxed atmosphere for its guests. TAYLOR COLLECTION

GLACIER NATIONAL PARK HOTELS

GLACIER NATIONAL PARK

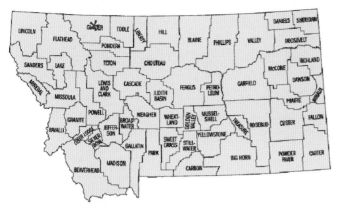

Scattered among the rugged peaks, jagged rocks, the rumbling creeks and alpine lakes of Waterton-Glacier International Peace Park stand many architectureal treasures. These buildings are remembrances of one man's vision, and they have reached the hearts of millions of visitors.

By 1891, the Great Northern Railway's Marias Pass route, skirting the southern border of what would become Glacier National Park, was a brand new addition to Montana. The territory had gained statehood only two years previously, and tourism was not yet a byword, but

Louis W. Hill

the seeds were being planted that would make tourism a future Montana industry.

Louis W. Hill became president of the Great Northern Railway in 1907. He saw his railway

and the potential establishment of Glacier National Park as two interlocking puzzle pieces. Glacier became a national park in 1910, creating for Hill the perfect destination for Great Northern touring car passengers. Hill began to tailor the railroad's advertising campaigns, taking tourists westward. Slogans such as "See America First" and "The National Park Route" encouraged Americans to look inward instead of abroad for recreational possibilities. The railroad opened up the"frontier," and those with even a small spark of curiosity came to see the acclaimed sites. In many ways, the Great Northern Railway made Glacier National Park an overnight success.

Hill knew the wealthy clientele he attracted would expect exceptional accommodations, with the Great Northern's ready access to the park. Because there was only one hotel inside the park, the Lewis Glacier Hotel (now Lake McDonald Lodge), Hill needed to build other accommodations, especially on the eastern side. Constructing Glacier Park Lodge and several backcountry chalets was Hill's initial focus, with Many Glacier Hotel and the Prince of Wales Hotel to follow.

Glacier Park Lodge was completed in 1913, establishing the Great Northern's first park stop from the east. By the end of 1914, the Great Northern had built the largest hotel in the park, Many Glacier Hotel, as well as nine chalets. With the exception of Belton, the chalets were accessible primarily by boat or trail. Hill's last structure, the Prince of Wales Hotel, was completed in Alberta, Canada in 1927, thus setting the stage that would bring the two parks closer as Waterton-Glacier International Peace Park on June 18, 1932.

The ownership of the hotels and chalets (excluding Lake McDonald Lodge) has changed twice since the Great Northern Railway constructed and began operating them in 1912.

In 1961, the hotels and chalets were sold to independent owner Don Hummel, and operated as Glacier Park Incorporated. Under a 25-year contract the concessions were sold again in 1981 to a subsidiary, Dial Corp. (formerly known as Greyhound Corporation). The Viad Corp. now owns The Glacier Park Company. The Great Northern Railroad is still remembered as founder of the concessions in Glacier. Today the Waterton-Glacier International Peace Park contains four concessioner hotels, two chalets, three campstores and three motor inns.

TEXT FROM BRIDGET MOYLAN'S, *GLACIER'S GRANDEST*

LOBBY, GLACIER HOTEL. LAKE MC DONALD, MONT.

The Lobby is the most architecturally significant space in the Lake McDonald Lodge. The concrete floors are scored in imitation of flagstone and have incised messages in Blackfeet, Chippewa and Cree that translate into phrases such as "welcome," "new life to those who drink here," "looking toward the mountain" and "big feast." GLACIER NATIONAL PARK PHOTO, T.J. HILEMAN COLLECTION

The front side of
Lake McDonald
Lodge faces the lake.
GLACIER NATIONAL PARK
PHOTO

The back side of Lake
McDonald Lodge faces
the entrance road. GLACIER
NATIONAL PARK PHOTO, R.E.
MARBLE COLLECTION

A postcard view of Glacier Park Lodge in 1913, a year before the south annex was added. Total cost of the entire hotel was $500,000.

The spacious lobby in the Glacier Park Lodge.

This panoramic view shows the massive timbers used in construction of Glacier Park Lodge.

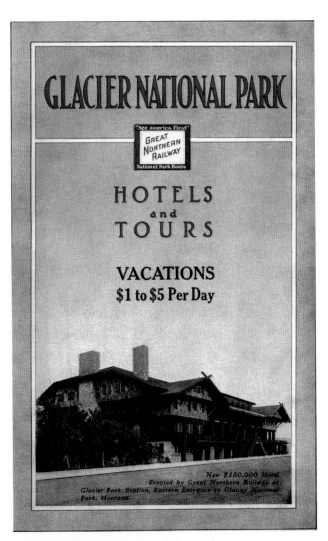

The magnificent lobby of the Many Glacier Hotel was decorated in an Oriental theme in the 1920s. Until 1957 a circular staircase and fountain were in the lobby.

A 1913 guide to the hotels of the Park. TAYLOR COLLECTION

The Many Glacier Hotel is at the end of a 12-mile road in the Many Glacier Valley on Swiftcurrent Lake. It was opened on July 4, 1915, and is the largest hotel in the park. An annex was added in 1917. In 1918 the hotel had a swimming pool, tailor shop, barber shop, hospital, telephones, hot and cold running water and steam heat.

"Go to Glacier now and tramp or ride her wilderness trails and surroundings repeated nowhere else on earth. Camp by the way, or stop at chalets...above all, take time. At Swiftcurrent Lake one can pass days and weeks without leaving the environs of Many Glacier Hotel in contemplation of mountains, lakes and glaciers, which yield Glacier's inmost secrets..." *National Parks Magazine,* 1946. MHS #956-689

1930s White tour buses stop at the entrance to Many Glacier Hotel as bellmen greet the guests. GLACIER NATIONAL PARK PHOTO

A 1920s view of the Many Glacier Hotel dining room with Great Northern Railroad's Oriental theme. GLACIER NATIONAL PARK PHOTO, HILEMAN COLLECTION

THE GRAND HOTEL

BIG TIMBER

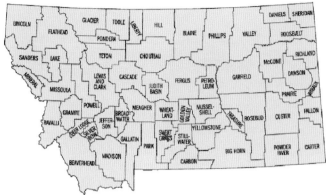

THE GRAND HOTEL
BED AND BREAKFAST
BOX 1242
MCLEOD STREET
BIG TIMBER, MT 59011
1-406-932-4459
8 ROOMS, 1 APARTMENT AND 1 SUITE

Big Timber in Sweet Grass County had its major growth period after 1883 when the Northern Pacific Railroad established a depot. Within 10 years, the community became the business center for a large surrounding area. It also became the largest wool shipment point in Montana, a shippin g point for sheep, cattle and horses, and an outfitting center for the mining industry up the Boulder River.

With such prosperity in the area, it made sense to replace the town's log structures with new masonry buildings along McLeod Street, Big Timber's commercial thoroughfare. One building was built by the Halvorson brothers in 1890 and named The Grand Hotel. The brothers were very successful in the sheep trade and spent $20,000 on their sandstone and brick hotel.

Originally there were eight ground floor rooms and 30 upstairs, a restaurant, saloon and game room. Room rates were $1.00 per night or $1.25 with a telephone. An 1898 newspaper article stated the hotel closed for a year during the Panic of 1893 and that in 1898, the hotel was upgraded at a cost of $2,500 and room rates had risen to $2 to $2.50 per night. A barber shop and billiard room had been added. The hotel became known along the Northern Pacific Rail-

road (the main means of traveling in those days) as one of the best managed and best equipped hotels along the line of the road.

The hotel survived the great fire of March 13, 1908, when more than a third of the town was razed. Over the years there were several noticable changes to the building. The stairway in the parlor was rotated 90 degrees in 1907 and, in 1914, a canopy was added which extended over the McLeod Street sidewalk. That same year an addition was added at the rear, or east end of the hotel.

The hotel had many owners through the years and many interior remodelings including removal of the sidewalk canopy. It continued to cater to visitors from all over the world and like many other Montana hotels had visits from a variety of celebrities including actors Jeff Bridges,

Angela Lansbury and pianist, Peter Duchin. There were many stories told about the Grand through the years. Here's one told by Sandi Blake:

Sim Roberts, a notorious character in these parts in the late 1800s, is linked to the history of the Grand Hotel by an incident which happened there about 1894. According to Nat Clark, a longtime local rancher with a keen memory, his father, Jack, became acquainted with Sim under rather unusual circumstances. As Nat relates it:

"This desperado, Sim, had just killed a man on Main (McLeod) Street, and the dead men's buddies turned around and shot the offender. He was hauled into the Grand all shot up. Dr. Moore and Father were playing pool, and when they brought the man in, they put a couple of sheets on the pool table, laid him out and the doctor proceeded to get the lead out. The doctor asked my father to administer the chloroform

and whether due to the fumes or the blood–he never knew–my father passed out before the desperado did! When he came to, the operation had been a success. When they were finished they put the desperado in a room upstairs and my dad took care of him, and they became life-long friends."

In 1895, the hotel was extensively remodeled and has since become widely known for its food and wine list. Owner Larry Edwards takes pride in winning the prestigious Wine Spectator Award of Excellence every year since 1992. The Grand became the first restaurant in Montana to win the award, which is sponsored by the magazine, *Wine Spectator* in 1992. Edwards says "Our wine list is strictly American. That way we can concentrate on some great wines rather than offering an eclectic scattering of wine from around the world." His wine selection, which is housed in the hotel's basement at a year round temperature in the mid to high 50s, is so well-known that wine distributors and even vineyard owners come to Big Timber to do their staff training.

But wine and food are only a part of this quaint hotel. There are eight rooms, one apartment and one large suite, all uniquely appointed in 1890s decor and a totally restored 1890 saloon.

This ad reflects the times.

The Grand Hotel on McLeod Street, circa 1924. CRAZY MOUNTAIN MUSEUM

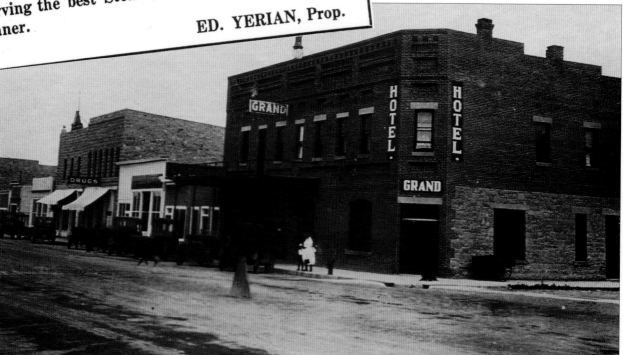

Hotel ledger from June 1898.

CHRISTMAS AT THE GRAND MENU, 1911
(as published in the Pioneer Newspaper)

Hors 'dOeuvres
Olives et Anchovies   Chow Chow
Caviar

Pottage
Tete de Veau en Torture
Cream Chicken ala Princess
Poisson
Fried Smelts, Anchovy Sauce

Entrees
Velau vent of Calves Brains, Raveote
Stuffed Eggs ala Nige
Riz de Veareaut Truffes
Bonchies ala Reine

Roasts
Tenderloin of Beef au jus
Tenderloin of Veal Burneace Sauce
Young Goose, Oyster Dressing
Giblet ala Nagout   Pork, Apple Sauce
Chicken, Cranberry Sauce
Pommes de Terre frites asparagus
Petit Pois   Pommes de Terre

Entrements
Creme de Cafe   Galeau de Framboises
Gelee de Punch   Eufs ala Apricot
Fromage de Creme Celeri
Boiled Suet Pudding ala Anglaise
Brandy sauce

Big Timber Pioneer,
March 29, 1892.

THE GRAND UNION HOTEL

FORT BENTON

THE GRAND UNION HOTEL
1 GRAND UNION SQUARE
BOX 1119
FORT BENTON, MT 59442
1-406-622-1882
1-888-838-1882
GRANDUNION@3RIVERS.NET
WWW.GRANDUNIONHOTEL.COM
27 ROOMS
RESTAURANT AND LOUNGE
GROUP FACILITIES

The birthplace of Montana is a small town on the banks of the Missouri River in Chouteau County. Fort Benton was a fur trading post first and being at the head of navigation on the Upper Missouri River, it became the hub for trade and travel for all of Montana and parts of western Canada. Although the town was established in 1846, Lewis and Clark had come through the area 40 years before. Mountain men such as Jim Bridger, Kit Carson and John Colter roamed the area.

But it was the steamboat that built the town. Thousands came up the river seeking their fortunes. Tons of fur and gold were shipped out. The first Blackfeet Indian agency was established here and Montana's first white child was born here. During the Montana gold rush, 50 steamboats a season docked with passengers and supplies, including whiskey, which found its way up the infamous Whoop-up Trail to Canada.

The demise of the town as a bustling commercial port started in the early 1880s when railroads in Canada and Montana stretched their tracks across the country, bypassing Fort Benton. Only four boats tied up at the wharves in 1888 and

the last commercial cargo arrived in 1891. In 1965, Fort Benton was granted national acclaim as a National Historic Landmark for the important part it played as the head of navigation on the Missouri River and the opening of the Northwest and western Canada.

The Grand Union Hotel, located on Front Street, has been called the "most historic edifice in the State." Construction was started in 1881 and opened on Nov. 2, 1882, with the biggest party the city and territory had ever seen. Over 300 attended including some of the most prominent men and women in Montana's history.

A group of local men organized the Benton Hotel Company to finance a $50,000 building and $150,000 in furnishing. William H. Todd had the hotel under lease. The building is three stories high and measures 115'x85' and used about 500,000 red bricks manufactured in a kiln below the present train depot. The name of the hotel represents the reconciliation of the nation following the Civil War in which many of the guests had participated.

Unfortunately the hotel opened just one year before the Great Northern Railway finished its line across Montana. Although the town's business suffered, the hotel continued in business with a succession of owners and managers. In 1899, the hotel closed for three months for extensive remodeling, including steam heat installation, electric lights and refinishing. In 1917, Charles Lepley bought the hotel and operated it until his death in 1941. His wife continued the operation until 1951.

The town and hotel went through many up and down years of business and Prohibition dealt a blow to the hotel bar business from which it briefly recovered in the 1930s. Later the building housed a ladies' store and, after World War II, an army surplus store. It ended up as a flop house and then was divided up for office space and finally sat abandoned.

In 1995, Jim and Cheryl Gagnon bought the dilapitated building and after a $1.5 million restoration and seven months of work, reopened the hotel on Nov. 13, 1999. Jim was a corporate business consultant and former bank executive, and Cheryl was a commercial designer so they were a natural match for this large restoration project. The ornate chimneys on the roof had been taken off in the 1960s by then owner Harold Thomas, who kept the old hotel from being razed. Luckily the original staircase, front desk and wainscoting were still intact. Even the original safe was still in the building. The original 55 very small rooms have been reduced to 26 in various configurations. An award-winning restaurant and a bar add to the ambience of one of Montana's most historic buildings.

Modern views of the ornate brickwork on the hotel building.

MODERN-DAY VIEWS OF THE GRAND UNION HOTEL

The Union Grille Restaurant is on the ground floor overlooking the Missouri River..

The saloon at one time was turned into a ladies dress shop and later headquarters for the local draft board.

The Lewis & Clark Room is located on the ground floor just off the lobby. It is ideal for meetins or special dinner occasions.

The lobby desk from 1882 is restored with faux-wood paint over softwood in keeping with the originals. Hardwood was too expensive to bring upriver in the 1880s.

Rooms and suites are done in period furniture as well.

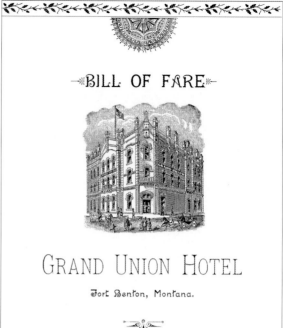

Menu

Platt's Select Raw
Puree of Chicken.   Mock Turtle.
Baked Salmon, Tomato Sauce.
Potato Croquettes.
Salmi of Prairie Chicken.
Sweet Breads Larded with French Peas
Chicken Liver Omelette
Pine Apple Fritters.
→UNCLE • TOBY • PUNCH←
Sirloin of Beef with Brown Gravy
Roast Sucking Pig with Bread Dressing
Apple Sauce.
Roast Young Turkey, Cranberry Sauce
Saddle of Venison • Haunch of Elk
With Currant Jelly.

Menu

Chicken Salad.   Shrimp Salad.
Dressed Celery.
Cold Corned Beef   Ham.
Mashed Potatoes.   Garden Peas.
Sweet Corn on Cob.
Hot Slaw.
Mince Pies.   Lemon Cream Pies.
Cranberry Pies.
English Plum Pudding, Rum Sauce
Assorted Cake.   Confectionery.
Vanilla Ice Cream.
Fruit.   Nuts.
Edam Cheese.   Coffee

This is quite a menu for an 1880s Christmas Eve dinner in the dining room of the Grand Union Hotel.

→BILL OF FARE←

GRAND UNION HOTEL

Fort Benton, Montana.

James & Cheryl Gagnon Proprietors

The hotel in the 1880s. A "Ladies Entrance" was on the northwest side of the building. "Real ladies of the West should not have to walk through the hotel lobby (which was littered with spittoons and tobacoo chewing roughnecks) or past the open door to the saloon." SCHWINDEN LIBRARY, FORT BENTON

A 1920s view of the hotel. The World War One statue, the first one dedicated in Montana in 1921, was moved in the 1950s to the American Legion Park after being damaged by an automobile. SCHWINDEN LIBRARY, FORT BENTON

When the hotel opened, the *Benton Record* described the lobby's desk as "one of the finest hotel counters in Montana." It is 16-feet long on its longest side, then curves back six feet and upon it is stained glass set in a frame, and an aperture through which the clerk can see all that is going on and receive payments.

View of the dining room showing the ladies' staircase at the right and over the rear doors, the window from the secret spy chamber.
SCHWINDEN LIBRARY, FORT BENTON

The hotel's saloon on May 13, 1936. SCHWINDEN LIBRARY, FORT BENTON

HOTEL BECKER

HARDIN

HOTEL BECKER BED & BREAKFAST
200 NORTH CENTER
HARDIN MT 59034
1-406-665-2707
1-406-665-3074
SEVEN ROOMS
BREAKFAST

The townsite of Hardin, in Custer County, was platted in 1907. That year, 25 men from Billings came by train to purchase lots. A German native, Anton Becker, was one of them. He purchased a lot at what would become the corner of Center Avenue and 2nd Street. Becker's family moved to Hardin in 1908 and into the upstairs of a two-story brick building that Becker had built known then as the Montana Saloon. He bought additional lots adjacent to the saloon.

For the next few years the town grew, more businesses were established and by 1917, the streets were being paved. That year Becker started building a large three-story building, incorporating his saloon and costing $60,000. It would be Hardin's second hotel and opened on June 28, 1918. An opening ad stated: "We wish to announce to the public that Hotel Becker is complete, all outside rooms. Mr. and Mrs. A. Becker are conducting it in a strictly first class manner. Rates from $1.00 and up."

The new building had a large lobby on each of the three floors, a barroom, dining room, kitchen and parlor. There were 38 rooms, some with a private bath. The *Hardin Tribune* called it one of the most modern hostelries in the state. The hotel was a gathering place for local ranchers, farmers and salesmen, who would show their wares to the local businesses.

Anton Becker died in 1920 and his widow, Katie, left for California where she stayed for 10 years. She leased out the hotel or hired a manager until 1930 when she returned to Hardin. Mrs. Becker died in 1942 and her daughter and son kept the hotel until finally selling it in 1954 for $42,000. The hotel went through several

owners until local resident, Mary Slattery, bought the building and turned it into a seven-room bed and breakfast on the first and second floors.

No longer can cowboys ride their horses into the bar and no more setting mattresses on fire by careless smokers (the hotel is non-smoking). It is a convenient stopping place for travelers to the area visiting Little Big Horn Battlefield, the Big Horn River as well as Crow and Northern Cheyenne reservation activities.

An early 1900s view of the Hotel Becker on the corner of Center Avenue and 2nd Street.
BIG HORN COUNTY HISTORICAL SOCIETY

HOTEL CALVERT

LEWISTOWN

HOTEL CALVERT
216 7TH AVENUE SOUTH
LEWISTOWN MT 59457
1-406-538-5411
WWW.TEIN.NET/~CALVERT
45 ROOMS

The settlement of central Montana, with Lewistown as its hub, came about with the Federal Homestead Acts of 1901 and 1912. These provided for 320 acres of free land and a three-year waiting period. With the Chicago, Milwaukee & St. Paul Railroad reaching the Judith Basin area in the early 1900s, the settlers began to arrive by the thousands. this brought a great amount of construction to Lewistown.

Education was a priority for the early settlers and with the great distances involved in this part of Montana, school children had to come to town and stay during the school year. Adequate housing was at a premium because of the rapid growth and boarding houses were few and very expensive.

In 1915 the local school administrator recommended that a dormitory be built for the out-of-town students. The next year the school joined with the local Chamber of Commerce to raise the needed funds. The Central Montana Improvement Corporation was formed, and with the local business community, raised $30,000 by sale of stock.

The dormitory was built on 7th Avenue South in 1917, made of native brick rising two-and-one-half stories, with 27 rooms for about 50 students. It had a full kitchen, dining room and laundry on the lower floor, with rooms for boys on the main floor, and a parlor and rooms for girls on the top floor. This is presently the south side of the hotel. An addition was added on the north side around 1919 doubling the rooms, increasing the size of the dining room, kitchen and staff quarters and adding a two-room infirmary. This is the build-ing which the hotel occupies today.

The economy of the region drastically declined in the 1920s because of drought and the exodus of people after World War One. The dormitory closed in 1925 and remained closed until Mrs. Emma Marsh purchased it in 1928. She and her husband, George, began the conversion to a hotel, adding many private bathrooms and a considerable amount of quality furniture. Mr. Marsh has previously owned Lewistown Furniture Company.

John and Eleanor Humphrey purchased the hotel in 1978 and have extensively renovated the building. Rooms, hallways and lobbies have been redecorated, and where possible, furniture has been refinished. Some of the 45 rooms contain original dormitory furniture, some have furniture the Marsh's brought in, and some contain furniture from the Brooks Hotel, which was on Main Street.

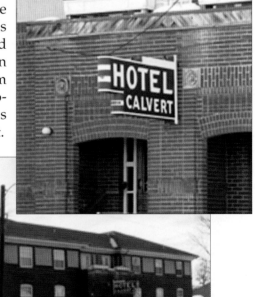

HOTEL LINCOLN

LINCOLN

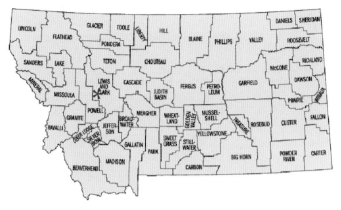

HOTEL LINCOLN
BOX 1000
LINCOLN MT 59639
1-406-362-4396
RESERVATIONS@HOTELLINCOLN.NET
14 ROOMS
RESTAURANT AND BAR

The original town of Lincoln, in Lewis and Clark County, was a bustling placer gold mining camp during the mid- to late-1860s. It was located in Lincoln Gulch about three miles west of the present townsite. By the early 1870s, the gold had played out and the miners left, but settlement had started in Lincoln. The first building erected in the new community was a log structure known as the "Half-Way House Hotel." It was used as a temporary living quarters, later becoming an overnight boarding house for tourists.

In 1918, Leonard Lambkin moved from Great Falls, purchased the "Hotel," and with his brother, established Camp Lincoln in the Rockies, an early dude ranch. In 1925, tourist cabins were built on the property and the community was advertised as a prime vacation area for hunting and fishing.

The area was also one of artist Charlie Russell's favorite places. As the story goes he would trade his pencil sketches to the bartender for display on the bar's walls. Unfortunately the sketches were lost when the bar burned down in the 1950s. In 1929, Lambkin erected a two-story lodge adjacent to the original hotel (which was moved in the 1950s). The building was 32'x80' and had 11 rooms and one bathroom on each floor. Its architecture is an excellent example of a vernacular Rustic design influenced by the Adirondack Rustic style, popularized in the Adirondack region of northern New York from 1870 to 1930.

The hotel with a newer addition and alterations has had many owners since the Lambkin family sold out years ago. The Mercer Family (Larry, Julie and Marshal) from Evergreen, Colorado bought the property in 2002 and now call it the Hotel Lincoln. They offer three two-room suites and 11 regular singles along with an excellent restaurant and bar. Lincoln is 70 miles northeast of Missoula on Highway 200 in the heart of both summer and winter outdoor activities.

Camp Lincoln *in the* Rockies

AT Lincoln, Montana, in the Big Blackfoot Valley, a 25-room frame hotel, electrically lighted, semi-modern and comfortable is surrounded by 12 neat rustic cabins. Here 150 guests can be entertained, enjoying 160 acres of forest and valley country surrounded by the main range of the Rockies. Saddle horse trips to distant peaks, lakes, abandoned mining camps and pack trips of 12 days through virgin country to Glacier National Park are features of Camp Lincoln. The largest pine trees in Montana grow in this valley. Copper Lake is 9 miles away, Silver King Lake, 10 miles distant, and Hart Lake, 16 miles from camp. Native and silver salmon trout are caught in these lakes. Within 3 miles of the hotel are 12 good fishing streams.

Hiking, big game hunting, dancing in the log dance pavilion and nightly camp-fires keep guests busy in addition to fishing and riding.

A Gateway to Glacier Park *via* Pack Trails

The Glacier Park 12-day pack trip and other shorter trips of from 1 to 10 days into the mountains to the north allow tourists a wonderful experience.

Camp accommodations are excellent. Bathing facilities and out-door sanitary toilets are convenient. Spring water supplies the cabins and a laundry is on the grounds.

Rates

$6 a day, $40 a week and $150 a month with half rates for children under 12 years and special rates for families include the use of a horse, saddle and blanket. There are special rates for the pack trips and hotel cost is deducted while guests are on such trips. Transportation in the hotel bus or stage from Helena to Lincoln (50 miles) costs $3.50. S. J. Lambkin is the hotel proprietor. Season: June 1 to November 1.

You Will Never Be the Same!

A ROCKY MOUNTAIN vacation does something to you! The change is permanent, too—you'll enjoy it for the rest of your days.

City routine may rob you of your mountain appetite. The wind-and-sun tan may fade. But you'll still be a different person after a real adventure in the Rockies—different for life!

After the Dude Ranch, for instance, there will be a longing you never knew before—for jagged skylines, tumultuous streams, glorious hours of physical exertion, the everlasting presence of the mountains, snowy clouds drifting across a Montana or a Wyoming sky!

We believe you'll want different things, you'll like different people, demand different kinds of fun! You will be a freer, surer, more interesting person. You'll even like yourself better after a Rocky Mountain vacation. Find out this summer what the Rockies can do for you.

A "Dude Ranch" Vacation Will Never be Forgotten

Let us show you our country—mountain trails winding high, deep-set lakes and streams teeming with fighting, leaping trout, color in the rocks, the sky, the snow and the trees! Let us bring to you the lore of the old picturesque West, of the days when mountaineering was known only to the hardy pioneer and the Indian.

Come!

If you want to settle back and rest, gathering new strength and health from the wholesome air of this region, you will find our quarters exceptionally comfortable, homelike, clean. If you want exercise, here is the place to get it.

Make next summer a "Dude Ranch" summer! Begin to plan now!

1—A "dude" cabin at Lincoln.

2—Lincoln, Montana.

3—The town of Lincoln is typically western.

4—A log dance pavilion where nightly camp fires and parties are held.

5—Fishing on the Big Blackfoot River.

One of the two-room suites.

Miss Kitty's is decorated in simple, rustic style.

The bar looking toward the dining room.

The corridor in the historic part of the hotel with rooms on both sides.

Miss Kitty's Restaurant serves mainly dinners in the steakhouse-style. Breakfasts are also available.

HOTEL MONTANA

REED POINT

HOTEL MONTANA
201 NORTH DIVISION
REED POINT, MT 59069
1-406-326-2288
FIVE ROOMS PLUS BUNKHOUSE
BAR AND FOOD

One of the most unusual historic hotels in Montana has to be the Hotel Montana in the small town of Reed Point in Stillwater County. The hotel occupies a building built around 1909. Reed Point today has about 100 residents, but in its boom years (early 1900 to the late 1920s) it had over 50 businesses and three banks.

The hotel building had a number of occupiers before being converted to a hotel in 1997. It started out as a mercantile store with the owners living upstairs along with offices for a lawyer and a doctor. In the 1920s and '30s the upstairs was a boarding house for local students and teachers. Then it was a general store plus three apartments until 1992.

In 1995, Russ and Connie Schuerert purchased the building and converted the lower area to a bar and the upstairs to five hotel rooms. Since they were in the antique business, the building has been decorated with their collec-

tion. The back bar came from the Wagon Wheel Saloon in Greycliff which closed in 1983.

Behind the hotel is an old bunkhouse that sleeps 10. It was brought in from a local ranch and later it was found out that it had originally been located in town and then moved to the ranch. Also out back is a unique two-story outhouse of the type that was there until 1937. The story goes that some kids pulled a prank and stole the outhouse and put it on a flat car on the nearby railroad siding. Unfortunately the car was hooked up to a freight train and the outhouse wound up in the Missoula railroad yards and was never returned. The building's owners built a new two-story outhouse for the boarders' use.

It is worth pulling off the freeway at the Reed Point exit to see this unique Montana treasure.

Izaak Walton Inn

Essex

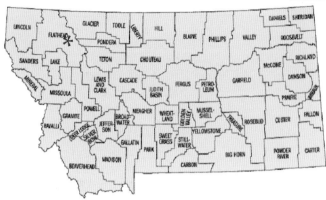

Izaak Walton Inn
290 Izaak Walton Inn Road
Essex, MT 59916
1-406-888-5700
stay@izaakwaltoninn.com
33 rooms
4 cabooses
restaurant & lounge

The newest of the Great Northern Railroad hotels is the Izaak Walton Inn, located at Essex on U.S. Route 2 in Flathead County, on the southern edge of Glacier National Park.

Essex is a small railroad town mainly consisting of a railroad yard with many tracks. It is on the west side of the Continental Divide (Marias Pass) and helper engines stand ready to help freight trains over the pass. The hotel was built in 1939 for the railroad to house their workers. At the time it was thought a third entrance to the park would be at Essex and the building could also be used as a hotel for tourists. The third entrance, however, never materialized due to finances and wartime conditions.

The hotel was named after Sir Izaak Walton, a 16th century English author and sportsman who wrote the book, *The Compleat Angler*. James Willard Schultz, who lived in the area, probably named the hotel. He was an author who fought alongside the Blackfeet Nation until they were confined to their reservation. Schultz convinced the railroad to rename sites along their route to better reflect the area's history and culture.

There was a ranger station in the 1930s named the Izaak Walton Ranger Station and at one time Essex was named Walton, so in 1939, it made sense to name the new hotel the

Izaak Walton Inn. Before the hotel was built the railroad crews had to live in outfit cars and in the winter it was hard to get crews to live and work in such harsh conditions. The railroad finally decided that a substantial building was needed at Essex (Walton) to house their crews and in April 1939 made a contract with the Addison Miller Company to build and operate a hotel and lunchroom on railroad land at Essex (still named Walton at this time).

The hotel was opened on Nov. 1, 1939. It had cost $40,000 to construct and was two-and-one-half stories, 36' by 114' and had 29 rooms, 10 bathrooms, a large lobby, dining room, kitchen and several other service rooms including a general store. Although the hotel operated at a loss for years, the Addison Miller Company continued to run it until around 1957 when it sold out.

Several owners continued to operate the Inn

for the next 25 years until the present owners, Larry and Lynda Vielleux purchased the property in 1982. Since then they have upgraded the facilities and have built essentially a year-round business with tourists in the summer months and a major cross-country ski destination area in the winter. An added bonus to the business is the fact that the Inn is a railroad haven, with a working railyard just 50 feet from the front door.

A million acres of wilderness with jagged peaks, wildlife and glaciers await visitors to the Inn. There is hiking, fishing and wildlife viewing both in the park and the surrounding national forests. The Inn has 30 Empire Builder rooms with private baths, three Empire Builder family rooms and four original cabooses that offer a unique overnight stay. There is a lounge, an excellent restaurant and gift shop.

A 1940s view of the lobby and at left, a modern view. The Inn preserves its railroad heritage while offering country-style charm.

The back side of the hotel faces the Burlington Northern Santa Fe Railyard.

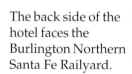

A LA CARTE		A LA CARTE	

Steak and Chops
(SERVED WITH TOAST, BUTTER, POTATOES and COFFEE)

Top Sirloin Steak	80	Hamburger Steak	40
T-Bone Steak	80	Veal Steak	60
Tenderloin Steak	80	Veal Cutlets . 60 breaded 65		
Sirloin Steak	65	Pork Chops ... 50 breaded 55		
Rib Steak	60	Pork Tender . 55 breaded 60		
Plain Steak	50	Pork Sausage	45
Salisbury Steak	45	Calves Liver, Bacon & Onions .. 50		
Veal Chops	60	Lamb Chops	50

Sandwiches
(DRINKS EXTRA WITH SANDWICHES: TOASTED; 5c EXTRA)

Cube Steak	40	Denver	35
Roast Beef ...... 15 Hot ... 25		Sardine	20
Roast Pork ...... 20 Hot ... 30		Tuna Fish	20
Baked Ham ..... 20 Hot ... 30		Lettuce and Tomato	25
Hamburger	20	American Cheese	15
Chicken Salad	35	Peanut Butter	10
Fried Egg	15	Club House, 3-decker	50

Cold Meat Suggestions
(SERVED WITH TOAST, BUTTER, POTATO SALAD and COFFEE)

Cold Beef or Pork	50	Assorted Cold Meats	
Boiled Ham	50	with Chicken	60
Assorted Cold Meats	50	Dutch Lunch	50

Eggs and Omelets
(SERVED WITH TOAST, BUTTER, POTATOES and COFFEE)

Boiled, Fried or Scrambled		Ham or Bacon and Eggs	50
Eggs (2)	35	Minced Ham & Scrambled Eggs 45	
Poached on Toast (2)	40	Plain Omelet	40
Poached Vienna Style (2)	60	Minced Ham or Bacon Omelet . 50	
Fried Ham	50	Spanish Omelet	50
Fried Bacon	50	Jelly Omelet	50
Ham Steak	60	Cheese Omelet	50

DESSERT — FOUNTAIN — BEVERAGE MENU ON BACK COVER
BOTTLED BEER AT POPULAR PRICES

—SORRY WE CANNOT BE RESPONSIBLE FOR LOST ARTICLES—

Salads
(SERVED WITH TOAST, BUTTER and COFFEE)

Lettuce Salad	25	Crab Salad	50
Lettuce and Tomato	35	Chicken Salad	50
Potato Salad	25	Lettuce and Egg	40
Combination Salad	40	Shrimp Salad	50
Pineapple-Cottage Cheese	40	Tuna Fish Salad	50
Waldorf Salad	40		

Mayonnaise or French Dressing-10c extra

Seafoods and Fish in Season
(SERVED WITH TOAST, BUTTER, POTATOES and COFFEE)

Grilled Salmon Steak	50	Western Oysters w. Cole Slaw	60
Grilled Halibut Steak	50	Western Oysters w. Milk Stew . 50	
Filet of Sole, Tartar Sauce	50	Western Oysters w. Cream Stew 60	
Norwegian Sardines	40	Cove Oysters w. Milk Stew ... 40	
Cold Cracked Crab	60		

Relishes

Ripe Olives	15	Green Onions or Radishes	10
Sweet or Dill Pickles	15	Crisp Utah Celery	20
Sliced Cucumbers	15	Sliced Tomatoes	15

Appetizers

Grapefruit Juice	10	Fresh Orange Juice	15
Tomato Juice	10	Pineapple Juice	10
Orange Juice (canned)	10	Sauerkraut Juice	10

Vegetables and Potatoes

Fried Onions	10	Cottage Fried	20
Stewed Tomatoes	15	Lyonnaise	15
String Beans	15	Hashed Brown	15
June Peas	15	Shoestring	20
Stewed Corn	15	American or French Fried	15
Asparagus	25	Julienne or O'Brian	20

DESSERT — FOUNTAIN — BEVERAGE MENU ON BACK COVER
BOTTLED BEER AT POPULAR PRICES

—SORRY WE CANNOT BE RESPONSIBLE FOR LOST ARTICLES—

Menu from the 1940s.

The four caboose cottages sit atop a scenic hill overlooking the Inn and the railyards. They are fully insulated and heated and offer accommodations for four including cooking and bath facilities.

A 1940 view of the hotel looking north. GLACIER NATIONAL PARK ARCHIVES HPF 8080, MAR

JACKSON HOT SPRINGS LODGE

JACKSON

JACKSON HOT SPRINGS LODGE
BOX 808
JACKSON, MT 59736
1-406-834-3151
HOTRESORT@JACKSONHOTSPRINGS.COM
WWW.JACKSONHOTSPRINGS.COM
12 CABINS, FOUR-PLEX APARTMENT
HUNTERS CABINS
RV SPACES, TENT SITES
RESTAURANT & BAR

It was on July 6, 1806, that the Lewis and Clark Expedition first saw the Big Hole Valley: at noon on July 7, they had their "noon day" lunch at the hot spring. The hot springs in Jackson are the first springs to be mentioned in western history, and they named this "Hot Spring Valley." Clark wrote that this was one of the most beautiful valleys he had seen. He gave a splendid description, called people's attention to the number of fur-bearing animals to be found, told of the wonderful grasses that covered the plains, and gave a fair estimate of its size.

The town of Jackson in Beaverhead County is located on Highway 278, 95 miles southwest of Butte and 48 miles west of Dillon. The town of about 50 people is dominated by the resort complex. The hot springs are the town's water source so cold water is hard to come by.

After Lewis and Clark passed by there were some reports of fur trappers visiting the area in the 1820s but it was not until 1884 that a man named Benoit O. Fournier claimed the springs. He built a house and a small plunge for the use of travelers going through the area. M.D. Jardine purchased Fournier's interests in 1911 and built a hotel and plunge on Jackson's main street (now Highway 278) and piped the hot water 1,300 feet from its source to the pool.

In 1950 Mr. and Mrs. John Dooling, a Wyoming rancher and a Proctor & Gamble heiress, bought the property and built a $400,000 large lodge constructed of logs and an oak wood interior. A massive stone fireplace, large dance floor and a variety of animal horns and antlers add to the rustice western charm. Next to the lodge is an outdoor artesian hot pool, 30' x 75'. The new lodge was originally named the Diamond Bar Inn and Jackson became a mecca for both winter and summer activities.

Doolings' son inherited the resort, cut the large lodge in half and moved a section to Dillon. Today the resort features the rustic lodge, bar, gourmet restaurant, outdoor hot pool, 12 cabins featuring fireplaces, a four-plex apartment, rustic hunter's cabins, RV spaces and tent sites. Monte and Inge Peterson have owned the resort since 1990.

The pool measures 30′ by 40′ and was once covered. The temperature is maintained at 96° to 98° F.

Modern front view of the lodge.

Interior view of the lodge in the 1950s.

Exterior rear view of the lodge in the 1950s.

KALISPELL GRAND HOTEL

KALISPELL

KALISPELL GRAND HOTEL
100 MAIN STREET
KALISPELL, MT 59901-4452
1-406-755-8100
1-800-858-7422
GRAND@KALISPELLGRAND.COM
WWW.KALISPELLGRAND.COM
38 ROOMS, TWO SUITES
TWO RESTAURANTS
BAR AND CASINO
CONTINENTAL BREAKFAST

From the very inception of the frontier hotel business, there emerged in the Flathead Valley a hotel known for its finer amenities, the Kalispell Hotel. In 1912, the Kalispell Hotel hosted the relatively well-to-do traveler at a charge of $2 per night. This was considered twice the going rate of other hotels at that time. However, being situated in the heart of Kalispell's downtown business district and offering such privileged services as running water, door locks, and wake-ups, the Kalispell Hotel rarely hung out its vacancy sign. The three-story brick structure, designed by Kalispell architect Marion Riffo and built by local contractor B. Brice Gilliland, has stood through the years as a silent sentinel to the changes in the Flathead Valley and downtown Kalispell. During World War I information about the war was shouted to crowds of people at the corner of First and Main. In 1919, the City of Kalispell installed a water fountain on the corner where the hotel still stands. The fountain emphasized the importance of the First and Main intersection. On weekend nights, the Opera House crowd would gather around the fountain and frequent the Hotel lobby.

Frank Bird Linderman, a noted writer, leased and managed the hotel from 1924 to 1926. Famed artist Charlie Russell and author Irvin S. Cobb were good friends of Linderman. On occasion, they took lunch together and then would saunter back to the hotel lobby's stuffed leather chairs where they would sit exchanging thoughts and stories of the West.

Linderman, who lived the life of a true plainsman, migrated up the Missouri and continued overland to settle in Kalispell. He later wrote books and novels that are eagerly sought after by book collectors across the country.

Through the years, a number of individuals have owned the hotel. In the 1930s, the hotel owners planned extensive renovations including the addition of a fourth floor and what would have been Kalispell's first passenger elevator. These renovations never occurred; however, between 1939 and 1941 the interior of the Kalispell Hotel was remod-

eled. According to a contemporary newspaper description: "...The modern hotel room of today has to be definitely different than that of some few years ago, as most of the traveling public of today carry radios and electric razors in its luggage, and demands box springs and inner spring mattresses for sleeping comfort. An entirely new plan of interior decoration has been carried out that is highly attractive to the eyes and gives the guest who steps within its hospitable doors an immediate feeling of physical well being and luxury as well as appealing to his aesthetic sense."

During more recent decades the hotel fell on hard times and was reduced to taking in weekly, monthly, and even hourly tenants. In 1989 a major renovation began that brought the hotel back to vibrant life. The 51 "bath down the hall" rooms that had rented for $120 to $150 per month were transformed into 40 rooms with private baths.

The hotel reopened to guests in 1991 while renovation of the lobby continued. Today, the sweep of the original lobby can be seen, including the original oak stairway and the high, pressed-tin ceiling.

Early in Kalispell's history there were eight downtown hotels. Today only one remains–the Kalispell Grand Hotel. Inside the gracious lobby, the Kalispell Grand still awaits its guests who can readily envision the life and history of a bygone era.

As guests make their way up the oak staircase, they find rooms furnished and well-appointed in the same Victorian-style cherrywood. The rooms are of varying sizes with privacy of utmost concern. All the rooms have private baths and showers, cable television with remote and telephones equipped with a dataport.

Another view of the lobby. BOB STEPHENS PHOTO

The grand oak staircase in the lobby area.
BOB STEPHENS PHOTO

The Kalispell Hotel in the 1920s. MHS #948-773

LOLO HOT SPRINGS
GRANITE HOT SPRINGS

LOLO

L olo Hot Springs in Missoula County is one of the most historic sites in the state and was tainted with criminal activity. Today there are two distinct resorts–Lolo Hot Springs and a few hundred yards to the east–Granite Hot Springs.

The entire area was well-known to the Indians long before Lewis and Clark passed through the area in 1805. The Indians used the springs as a meeting place and bathing spot; wild game used it as a mineral lick. The 33 members of the Corps of Discovery and their guide, Sacajawea, first reached the site on Sept. 13, 1805, and left a written record: "Passed several springs which I observed the deer, elk, etc., had made roads to, and below one of the Indians had made a hole to bathe. I tasted this water and found it hot and bad tasted. In further examination I found this water nearly boiling hot at the places it spouted from the rocks. I put my finger in the water, at first could not bear it in a second," Captain Clark.

Early explorers, trappers and prospectors would rendevous at the springs and around 1810, a trapper named Lawrence lived in the area (possibly the Graves Creek area). The Indians called him Lou Lou or Lo Lo, which eventually became Lolo. A crude road was built through the Lolo Creek Canyon in 1888 connecting the hot springs with the Bitterroot Valley and Missoula. The next year a branch line was laid through the Bitterroot Valley and tracks were laid up Lolo Creek Canyon, but only as far as Graves Creek.

An advertisement in the *Missoulian* dated Aug. 16, 1888, stated: "These springs are known throughout the Northwest for their health giving qualities...in a beautiful country, plenty game and fishing. Board, room, and bath, eleven dollars per week. Fare by coach to and from the Springs, five dollars."

The first hotel was built about 1900 and burned down in 1903. That same year, Missoula resident Paul Gerber bought the fledgling resort. He was an owner of the Highlander Brewery in Missoula and was well-known for his penmanship, photography and artwork. He left within a year, apparently deathly afraid of ticks which were common in the wooded areas of the resort. The Gerber family ran

The restaurant, bar and store on the right, The Fort at Lolo Hot Springs on the left.

the resort for many years, building the first swimming pool in 1918 and many other buildings, mud baths and even a cabin that was hoped to be a hospital.

During the Prohibition years, people would go to the springs to dance and drink bootleg whiskey. The Gerbers sold the resort to a group of Missoulians in 1964. By this time the road over Lolo Pass was opened through to Lewiston, Idaho. In the mid-1960s, an out-of-state entrepreneur convinced the owners to build an Olympic luge run, the only one in the United States at the time, just above the pool and cabins. Nothing came of this venture however.

In the 1980s, the new owners of the resort were arrested by Secret Service agents for counterfeiting money on the premises. In 1985, Bill Wiley, a rancher from Arizona, bought the now-boarded-up resort and rebuilt the 1926 hotel and moved several cabins from the Lolo Hot Springs site to the Granite

Hot Springs site. He split off the Lolo part of the resort in 1988 and turned the Granite site into a private retreat. As of this writing (2004) the Granite Hot Springs area consisting of the eight-room lodge (1926 hotel), 13 cabins and other buildings, and outdoor hot pool and 271 acres is for sale.

The Lolo Hot Springs area now has two separate businesses. The hot springs resort, owned by LHS Inc., has a bar, restaurant, indoor and outdoor hot springs pools and a campground. It caters to snowmobilers in the wintertime. In 1990, Ken and Nancy Hansen opened the Fort at Lolo Hot Springs and recently opened the Lolo Trail Center, a 6,000-square-foot Lewis and Clark exhibition center and gift shop.

The entire complex is located 25 miles west of Lolo on U.S. Highway 12 and seven east of Lolo Pass.

This photo was taken from the parking lot looking north, just west of the pool. Compare this photo with the top left photo on the next page which shows the old cabins.

The outdoor pool has a temperature of 94° F.

A post card view of the Hot Springs in 1908.

LO LO SPRINGS HOTEL DESTROYED BY FIRE

Popular Summer Resort Goes Up in Smoke---No Insurance---Origin of Fire Unknown---Humorous Features and Incidents.

Missoulian headline from September 1, 1903.

The covered pool in 1918. UM#88-84

Early 1900s view of present Lolo Hot Springs showing some of the cabins of the time.

The resort's first swimming pool was built in 1918. The left building was a "hot bath" house, the long building, a covered pool. The present pools are also at this site. UM #84-53

The hot springs complex in 1909. This area is now Granite Hot Springs. SHERRY LIERMAN COLL.

Herman and Sarah Gerber built this cabin at the resort (now Granite Hot Springs) for their daughter, Marian, in 1910. It is still standing. UM #84-60

The resort had two hotels but one burned in 1903. This hotel, on the left, just a short distance upstream from the present (1926) hotel building was built around 1903 and torn down in 1965. TOM MULVANEY COLLECTION

Guests on the hotel's porch.
UM #77-274

This may be Paul Gerber's first car and the first one to reach the resort, circa 1905.
UM #88-0080

View of the restored original 1926 hotel.

Interior of the lobby of the 1926 hotel.

View of the main resort complex. The entire area consists of 18 structures total, including the eight bedroom lodge, 13 cabins, a horse stable on the other side of Highway 12 and a total of 271 acres.

Part of the 13 cabins, some moved over from Lolo Hot Springs. Five of these have Jacuzzis and two have whirlpool baths.

The year-round natural hot springs pool next to the hotel was covered until the Wiley family removed the roof and walls.

LOST TRAIL HOT SPRINGS RESORT

SULA

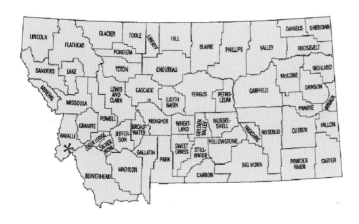

LOST TRAIL HOT SPRINGS RESORT
8321 HIGHWAY 93 SOUTH
SULA, MT 59871
1-406-821-3574
1-800-825-3574
LTHS@LOSTTRAILHOTSPRINGS.COM
10 CABINS
LODGE, MOTEL
OUTDOOR POOL/HOT TUB/SAUNA
RESTAURANT AND BAR
RV PARK

Lewis and Clark missed the hot springs six miles north of the pass that would be known as Lost Trail. They took a wrong turn which added a day and a half to their trek over the Bitterroot Mountains. It was not until almost 90 years later that a woman built a cabin near the springs so she could help her ailing son soak in the water.

The next owners, Mr. and Mrs. Frank Allen, decided to capitalize on the mining boom in nearby Gibbonsville in about 1895. Gibbonsville had blossomed to about 5,000 people, and the Allens decided to build a hotel. They constructed a two-story house with 14 rooms, but had not yet completed it when the mines ran out and the boom ended.

James Gallogly heard of the place through Mrs. Allen's mother and father, who he was boarding with in Gibbonsville. An assayer with the mines, he had enough money saved up to buy out the Allens' interest in 1897. The springs were still federal property, so Gallogly had five years to prove up on them. Lonely, he invited his sister, Mary A. "Polly" Gallogly to stay with him. Polly only had one arm, but was quite strong enough for the necessary work.

Work began on Highway 93 in 1935, and the road builders made camp at the springs. They also built a new road connecting the springs with the highway. James Gallogly also rebuilt the springs at this time.

A bathhouse and a residence were also constructed. In 1941, the pool, dining room and dressing rooms were built,

the pool being on the foundation of the original hotel. James died not too long after this and the pool was closed to the public for a time.

In 1954, the resort became a private boys camp which lasted into the 1970s, when it was opened to the public.

Today the resort is owned by Mary Dell Honey and consists of 10 modern cabins, the Sacajawea Lodge with 22 rooms and a bunk room, the Lewis Lodge Motel, a restaurant/bar combination, a large 25' x 75' outdoor pool with a year-round temperature average of 95° F. There is an adjoining indoor hot tub and sauna and an RV Park. The resort can sleep 150 people per night.

The resort is located six miles north of Lost Trail Pass on Highway 93 in Ravalli County and 88 miles south of Missoula. It is located in a rustic setting with downhill and cross-country skiing nearby.

The 10 cabins are all nestled in the large trees on the property. They all have bathrooms, kitchens, electric heat and queen-sized beds.

The dining room is decorated in a rustic style with a large stone fireplace. In the summer, one can dine on the deck overlooking the pool.

The pool and new lodge in the 1940s. This pool is covered by a dome in the wintertime with a water temperature of 92° to 94° F. It has a deep area and a 10-inch wading pool at the other. There is also a sauna and hot tub in the lodge building.

MADISON HOTEL

WEST YELLOWSTONE

MADISON HOTEL & GIFT SHOP
139 YELLOWSTONE AVENUE
WEST YELLOWSTONE, MT 59758
1-406-646-7745
WWW.MADISONHOTEL@WYELLOWSTONE.COM
22 ROOMS

One of Montana's small, charming historic hotels is located in the tourist town of West Yellowstone in Madison County.

In 1910, Roxey and Dolly Barttell arrived in West Yellowstone looking for work. Roxey found a job driving a stage coach from Monida to West Yellowstone. Dolly went to work in a café located on the site where their hotel would eventually be located. After working for two years, they had saved enough to build a little lodge next to the café, replacing a tent hotel.

The little lodge was hand-tooled and carved out of local lodgepole pine. It had six rooms upstairs, with a fireplace to keep it warm, and pitchers and bowls for water, which was hand-carried from a well at the Union Pacific Railroad depot across the street. Water wasn't piped into the hotel until the 1930s because Dolly felt it would make people lazy. The rooms were small, and there were no bathrooms inside, only chamber pots.

Downstairs was a lobby and a small area to write letters, play cards and work on hand projects, such as wood carvings, etc. Many people paid for their room with an exchange of animal skins and heads of their finished hand crafts.

In 1921, plans were made to expand the hotel with about 14 additional rooms, and a card room. Sadly, Roxey was hurt by a falling log during construction and died within two years. Dolly finished the expansion and later married a cigar salesman. They kept the hotel up and it became a favorite place for people to meet, especially during the long, cold winter months. The couple added electricity, running water in 1936, more rooms and a bar and dancehall.

In 1929, President Warren G. Harding stayed in the hotel during his visit to Yellowstone Park. President Herbert Hoover was also a guest along with Hollywood notables of the times such as Clark Gable, Wallace Berry and Gloria Swanson.

A.B. (Lon) and Grace Hadley purchased the hotel from Dolly in 1959. They opened up the downstairs rooms and established a large gift shop but the lobby and first six rooms as well as the upstairs remain original. The lobby is a charming experience full of authentic "Old Yellowstone" artifacts. Linda Christensen and Janet Ostler now greet customers during the season from late May to early October.

The hotel in the 1930s. YELLOWSTONE HISTORIC CENTER ARCHIVES

METLEN HOTEL

DILLON

THE METLEN HOTEL
5 SOUTH RAILROAD AVENUE
DILLON, MT 59725
1-406-683-2335
1-406-683-3544
METLENINFO@METLENHOTEL.COM
WWW.METLENHOTEL.COM
50 ROOMS
TWO BARS

The Metlen Hotel has, for close to 100 years, played a prominent role in the history of Dillon, Beaverhead County, as an architectural landmark dominating the downtown skyline and in the social lives of local citizens. One of the finest extant examples of commercial architecture built in the Second Empire style in the state, it pays tribute to a time when its owner and the community envisioned Dillon's rapid growth and development.

The hotel was constructed on the site of the Corinne Hotel, the first hotel in Dillon, which was described as a "flimsy structure, a combination of thin lumber, cloth-lined partitions, and other combustible materials. It had been transplanted along the railroad, having originally been down in Utah or Idaho." By the time of construction, Dillon was enjoying a position as the most significant railroad stop between Butte and the Idaho line and was well-established as a ranching and agricultural center. Gold mining in the area also contributed to the town's economic importance.

Joseph C. Metlen arrived in Montana in 1867 and with his brother settled on Horse Prairie and engaged in freighting from Corrine, Utah, to the gold fields at Bannock. Metlen became prominent in Beaverhead County in business and politics in the 1870s and '80s. He purchased the Corrine Hotel in 1884 and operated it until it burned down in 1892. He began construction of his new 60-room hotel in 1897 at a cost of $30,000.

It was a grand hotel for its day. It is two stories in height, with an additional story tucked under the gentle concave curve of the mansard roof, and built of sandstone and brick. An article from the Feb. 18, 1898, issue of the

Dillon Tribune tells of the grand opening:

"Amidst pomp and ceremony, the newly completed Metlen Hotel was opened to the public last Friday. The occasion was a memorable one and is the beginning of a new epoch in the history of Dillon.

"At the public reception given in the afternoon, the Dillon Brass Band was in attendance and opened the ceremonies with the well-known piece, 'A Hot Time in the Old Town Tonight,' that being the most appropriate selection that could be made.

"The reception rooms and parlors were artistically decorated with American Beauty roses, carnations and similax in profusion. The hostess, Mrs. J.C. Metlen, was assisted in receiving by her daughter, Mrs. John Howard of Butte, and Mesdames Hodgens and Fyhrie, Misses Long and Poindexter. From 2 to 5 the beautiful edifice was thronged with guests. The reception gowns worn by the ladies were in keeping with the beauty of all that sur-

rounded them. The hotel is beautifully furnished, and this fact escaped the notice of none.

"At 9 o'clock in the evening, The Metlen was crowded with guests. The first speaker to address the people was Gov. R.B. Smith, who paid high tribute to the city of Dillon and the enterprising gentlemen who had constructed such a fine institution as The Metlen in our midst. Chief Justice Pemberton next addressed the company in his usual jovial strain. After the speaking had been concluded, the Dillon Orchestra, under Prof. Sullivan, struck up the grand march. The march was led by Mrs. J.C. Metlen and Governor Smith, followed by Mrs. John Howard and Chief Justice Pemberton and Miss Carrie Metlen and J.C. Metlen. Dancing was then commenced and continued until the early hours of the morning.

"Over two hundred guests were present and the lovely gowns worn by the ladies lent much to the enchantment of the occasion. At midnight a tempting supper was served. Among the prominent out-of-town people who were present were Gov. R.B. Smith, Chief Justice Pemberton, Attorney General Nolan, State Auditor T.W. Poindexter, Hon. L.A. Walker, Hon. T.W. Collins, of Helena, H.J. Wilson of Butte.

"The Metlen is a fine, large, three-story brick building. In the basement is the furnace room, storeroom, club rooms, and tonsorial parlors. On the first floor is the office, bar room, public parlor, private parlor, bedrooms, bathroom, dining room, kitchen and sample room. On the second floor is the ladies' parlor, bedrooms, etc. The third floor consists entirely of bedrooms. The hotel is beautifully furnished throughout and possesses all the modern conveniences, such as steam heat, hot and cold water and electric lights.

"J.C. Metlen, the genial proprietor, is well-known all over Montana, having come here in the early '60s. He is an experienced hotel man, and understands the wants of the traveling public. The people of this vicinity have long felt the need of a first-class hotel, and should now do their part in maintaining the same. Mr. Metlen has best wishes of his friends throughout the state for the success of his new enterprise."

Metlen continued to operate the hotel until his death in 1906 and it continued to operate for many years although the business declined in the latter part of the 1900s due to changing travel conditions and the popularity of inexpensive motels on the periphery of Montana cities. In the mid-1990s local resident Sandra Ivenson came to the rescue of the old landmark. She is slowly bringing back the hotel to its 1890s look and has meticulously restored the rooms, mainly by herself. Most of the 50-some rooms have or will have original furniture and beds. The front bar still has the original call board and key rack and part of the original bar with beatle woodwork. In the back barroom is perhaps the most ornate and most valuable back bar in the state. It is worth a visit just to see the workmanship and Sandra is very proud of this artifact, which she installed in 1995, and the other historical memorabilia in the room. Although the restaurant is no longer open the bar is busy and if gaming is one's interest, live poker games can be found in the hotel bar.

It is a shame that there are not more people like Sandra in the state to save some of the hotel buildings that are still in existence.

Cornerstone set in 1897.

This photo was taken before the neon addition on the roof and the removal of the front balcony. The house next door, which is now the home of the hotel's owner, was built at the same time as the hotel. BEAVERHEAD COUNTY MUSEUM ARCHIVES, 111.11 M-7

This photo was taken in the 1950s after the neon sign was put in place and the balcony removed. BEAVERHEAD COUNTY MUSEUM ARCHIVES, 111.11 M-6

MONTANA HOTEL BED & BREAKFAST
BOX 423
ALBERTON, MT 59820
1-406-722-4990
MONTANAHOTEL@BLACKFOOT.NET
WWW.MONTANAHOTEL.NET
9 ROOMS
BREAKFAST

Thirty miles west of Missoula lies the railroad town of Alberton, straddling the Missoula-Sanders county line. When the Chicago, Milwaukee and St. Paul Railway (Milwaukee Road) was pushing west in 1909, it established the site of Alberton as a crew-change location and built this building to accommodate them. Passenger service ended in 1961 and the railroad shut down in 1974, leaving the hotel with few customers. The hotel was extensively remodeled and at one time housed a liquor store.

In 2000, Rebecca Haylitt and Steve Young bought the building and established the Montana Hotel, an eclectic bed and breakfast. The nine rooms have iron beds with Carolina quilts and shams, old oak dressers, and period decor, but also feature in-room phones, TVs and private baths. A full breakfast is offered and one can listen to Rebecca play the harp in this early 1900s atmosphere.

The comfortable lobby with its fireplace and homey dining room create a cheerful setting for delicious home-cooked meals. Antique and period light fixtures and furnishings enhance the early-century ambience. Diners look out on a large flagstone courtyard with a cool fountain grotto surrounded by a privacy fence. The hotel is open March-December.

The hotel was known in the early days as The Pioneer Saloon and Hotel.

THE MURRAY HOTEL

LIVINGSTON

THE MURRAY HOTEL
201 WEST PARK STREET
LIVINGSTON, MT 59047
1-406-222-1350
WWW.MURRAHOTEL.COM
29 ROOMS
LOUNGE

Located in Livingston, a town of 7,000 in Park County, The Murray is in the heart of movie star country and has had many stay in its rooms in the past few decades.

The original two-story hotel, at the corner of West Park and Second streets, was built in 1904 as the Elite Hotel and was owned by Josephine Kline. She was financed by the family of Senator James E. Murray of Montana. In the early days, the hotel had a lot of railroad business being right across the street from the Northern Pacific Railroad depot.

Even in its early years, the hotel had its share of celebrity guests including Buffalo Bill and Calamity Jane. In the 1920s, the hotel expanded to four floors and had the city's only elevator, a 1905 Otis hand-cranked model. But in the mid-1920s, the Murray family foreclosed on Mrs. Kline and took over the Elite, renaming it The Murray. In October 1934, Mrs. Kline and Mrs. Helen Sherwood hitch-hiked to Washington, D.C. to try and get President Roosevelt to help Mrs. Sherwood oust tenants from her farm near Livingston and also help Mrs. Kline get back her hotel which she contended was stolen from her. She apparently did not get the help she needed. For many years the hotel was considered one of the grandest in Montana and the Northwest.

The Murray's decline in the 1960s coincided with a growth in the Interstate highway system, a decrease in rail travel and the building of motels. In 1978, Cliff and Pat Miller, local ranchers, bought the hotel at an auction and revived it with new furniture, plumbing and decor.

In 1990, Dan and Kathleen Kaul, from the Twin Cities, discovered the hotel during a local skiing trip and bought it from the Millers the next year. Dan was a general contractor while Kathleen operated Subway franchises. From the original 66 rooms, they now offer 29 with original sinks, clawfoot bathtubs (only five have individual bathrooms) and antique furniture. On the left side of the hotel are the nicer rooms, two share a bathroom and the small, less expensive rooms are on the right side. The lobby has been refurbished keeping the original inlaid floor. The Murray Lounge, with its inlaid marble bar has been a hot spot for locals and the many artists, writers and movie stars who either live in the Livingston area or are there to shoot movies and commercials.

The list of movie celebrities reads like a Hollywood phone book. Sam Peckinpah, the well-known director, lived in the hotel from 1979 until his death in California in 1984. His suite was once occupied by Walter Hill, the son of James J. Hill, builder of the Great Northern Railway. The Murray also played

host to other notables such as the Queen of Denmark and humorist Will Rogers. Rogers and his buddy, Walter Hill, tried to bring a favorite saddle horse to Hill's third floor suite via the hand-cranked elevator. Peckinpah reportedly covered his windows with Mexican blankets and slept with a revolver and Bible on his nightstand (several bullet holes were found in his ceiling).

Movie stars such as Whoopi Goldberg, Rip Torn, Keith Carradine, James Woods, Peter Fonda, Jack Palance and Robert Redford have either stayed here or frequented the bar and restaurant, the Winchester (now closed).

View of the Elite hotel in the early 1900s. MURRAY HOTEL COLLECTION

The hotel cafe in 1912.
MURRAY HOTEL COLLECTION

A postcard view from the 1950s.

The layout and decor of the lobby has not changed much in the last 80 years.
MURRAY HOTEL COLLECTION

The Murray Hotel, located across West Park Street from the Northern Pacific Depot in the 1950s, view looking east.
MURRAY HOTEL COLLECTION

Bartender G. George in the lounge in 1937. Notice the slot machines on the right.
MURRAY HOTEL COLLECTION

Side view of the hotel looking south on Second Street in the 1930s. MURRAY HOTEL COLLECTION

One of the hotels most unusual guests was Robert Pershing Waldow, the tallest person in the world at 8'11.1". He was born in Alton, Illinois, in 1918. At age 13, he was 7'4" tall and by 18 was 8'4", weighed 390 pounds and wore a size 37 shoe. In 1937, Robert and his father made an extensive trip West and to Yellowstone Park as a goodwill ambassador for the International Shoe Company. The two (his father is on the left, owner James Murray on the right) stayed at the Murray. A car had to be modified so Robert could sit in the back seat and stretch out his long legs and in the hotel room, a special frame and three mattresses were put together to hold him. He was just barely able to get into the elevator by sitting down. His large feet troubled him for years and in July 1940, a fatal infection set in when a blister formed that would not heal. He passed away on July 15. He is buried in Alton with a statue to his memory in front of the Alton Museum of History and Art. MURRAY HOTEL COLLECTION

THE NORTHERN HOTEL

BILLINGS

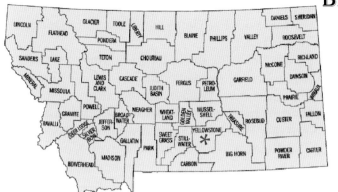

The majestic Northern Hotel at 19 North Broadway in Billings is one of only a few big city Montana hotels to still be operating as a hotel. The Northern is actually a result of a disastrous fire in 1940 that destroyed its predecessor, The Grand, at the same location.

The Grand Hotel and the city of Billings grew up together. It was built in 1904 by local businessmen, Preston B. Moss and Henry W. Rowley, and designed by well-known architect, J.G. Link. Moss was one of Montana's wealthiest men at the time. By 1904, Billings had a population of 10,000 and was the commercial center for southeastern Montana.

The hotel construction started with three stories and 69 rooms and, in 1916, a fourth story was added. Along with other additions the total number of guest rooms increased to 200. The total cost for the building had now reached $600,000. Room rates began at $1.50 per day and the hotel was the social center of town. Many dignitaries frequented the hotel, including Charley Russell and Teddy Roosevelt.

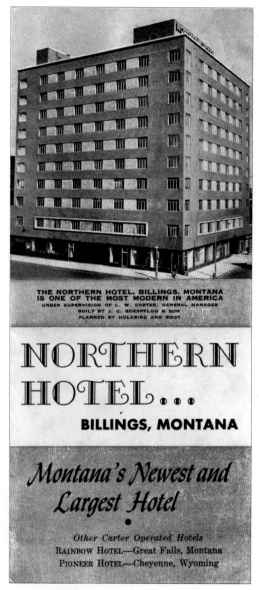

A 1942 brochure for the new hotel.

After Henry R. Rowley died in 1930, Moss operated the hotel with Mrs. Rowley until the night of Sept. 11, 1940, when the worst fire to occur in Billings up to that time broke out in the basement of the hotel and completely destroyed the building. Fortunately there were no casualties.

At the time, Moss was president of the Billings Investment Company. On the day after the fire, he was asked if he would "take the money and run." Mr. Moss, who was in his late 70s at that time, made a resounding commitment to rebuild the Northern (at some point the Grand had changed to the Northern) as the finest hotel in the West. The new hotel, built on the same site, was begun in April 1941 and opened on July 7, 1942, at a cost of one million dollars. The construction took place despite wartime shortages of building materials. At 10 stories, it was the tallest building in the state.

Les Carter, who was running the Hotel at the time, secured the operating lease for the new Northern Hotel when it opened. Carter, who was also president of the American Hotel Association, asked Western International Hotels to join in the operating lease, with the potential for the company to buy Mrs. Carter out in the event of his death. Carter did remain the manager until his death, at which time Western International Hotels assumed full management of the hotel.

In the fall of 1970, the hotel was purchased from the Moss and Rowley/Miller families by a group of local businessmen. Western International Hotels continued to manage the hotel for two years until the Northern Hotel Company assumed control. In 1981, the Genro Corporation of Denver, Colorado, became the general partner in the new ownership of the hotel. Hospitality Marketing and Management, Inc., took over management and in 1983 an extensive remodel took place.

Today the hotel has a beautifully restored lobby, 160 guest rooms, the Golden Belle Restaurant and Golden Belle Saloon, a fitness center and meeting space for groups up to 500 people. The hotel was a franchise of the Radisson Hotels and is now owned by the Yellowstone Hotel Group.

Post card view of the Northern prior to 1916.

A 1931 post card view of the hotel showing the 1916 fourth floor and rear additions.

The lobby of the old Northern Hotel.

The hotel the day after the Sept. 11, 1940, fire which destroyed the entire building. WESTERN HERITAGE CENTER, #84.13.94

A crowd in front of the hotel in honor of Crown Prince Olav and Princess Martha of Norway, June 2, 1939. Less than a year later, Norway would be occupied by German forces. WESTERN HERITAGE CENTER, #90.37.136, HART COLLECTION

Construction of the new 10-story hotel began in April 1941 and a grand opening was held on July 7, 1942. WESTERN HERITAGE CENTER

The Old Hotel

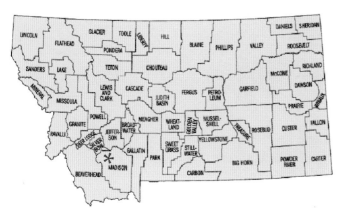

The Old Hotel on the corner of Fifth Avenue and Main Street in Twin Bridges in Madison County lives up to its name as it was built in 1879. It was first named Twin Bridge Hotel. The s was left off as a result of a sign painter's error. Bricks for the building were made on the Seidensticker Ranch. Mr. and Mrs. Owen Thomas, from Denmark, owned the hotel and had both overnight guests and boarders in the 11-room building.

Prior to the founding of Twin Bridges townsite by Mortimer H. Lott, Sr., the future town was a stage stop and mail drop at the intersection where the old road goes to Dillon.

When the hotel was built, the rooms had no clothes closets or central heating. Later two bathrooms were installed on each floor. Brass beds, commodes, dressers and tables were in each room.

Mr. and Mrs. Nicholls lived in the building starting in 1930 and reared 10 children there. In 1993, Scottish-born Jane Waldie purchased the building and opened it again as a bed and breakfast in 1996. The three-story building is now called The

Old Hotel and features two upstairs suites with a bedroom, private bath, separate sitting room and accommodates two or three guests. Her award-winning restaurant is known throughout the region and she caters to guests who come to fish the local streams. Jane's unique Scottish touches can be seen throughout the hotel and Highland flavorings can be tasted in her country cuisine. The Old Hotel is open May 1 through the end of October.

An 1893 view of the Twin Bridge Hotel.
JANE WALDIE PHOTO

OLIVE HOTEL

MILES CITY

THE OLIVE HOTEL
501 MAIN STREET
MILES CITY, MT 59301
1-406-234-2450
25 HOTEL ROOMS
34 MOTEL ROOMS
RESTAURANT
LOUNGE
CASINO

Since the 1880s, Miles City has been the trade, service and social center for the Eastern Montana area. After fire destroyed the well-known 1882 McQueen House in 1897, Miles City booster Joseph Leighton built "The Leighton" in 1898-99. In 1908, Maud and Albert Kinney bought the hotel and renamed it, "The Olive," after their daughter. The Chicago, Milwaukee and St. Paul Railway arrived the same year and the thriving economy encouraged the Kinneys to expand. Local architect Brynjulf Rivernes designed the new facade, lobby, and the east addition; a three-story addition arose to the rear. The lobby details are among the finest in the state, featuring high-quality oak woodwork and Rivernes' signature multi-colored tile flooring and curvilinear, clear, beveled glass window designs. The Olive now housed a cafe, barber shop, cigar and curio stand, buffet and sample rooms where ranchers and commercial travelers met. Two fireproof poured-concrete garages built in 1908 and 1912 demonstrate the rising importance of the automobile. The hotel remained a gathering place for townspeople and ranchers during the 1920s drought and the 1930s Depression. When agriculture and the economy rebounded after World War II, the hotel prospered again. The hotel now has 25 rooms, a lounge, dining room and casino. There is a 34-room motel annex across the street.

THE POLLARD

RED LODGE

THE POLLARD
2 NORTH BROADWAY
BOX 650
RED LODGE, MT 59068
1-406-446-0001
1-800-POLLARD
WWW.POLLARDHOTEL.COM
39 ROOMS
RESTAURANT AND LOUNGE

Frommer's guide book calls The Pollard Hotel in Red Lodge "one of the nicest hotels in the West-small, intimate and classy." The hotel was the first brick structure in the new coal mining town of Red Lodge in Carbon County. It opened as the Spofford Hotel in 1893, midway between the railroad depot and the populated section of town. It cost close to $20,000.

Thomas F. Pollard was one of Montana's and Red Lodge's most distinguished citizens. He was born in Omaha in 1866 and started working in the mines in Colorado in 1885 and two years later moved to Butte to work. Later he studied at the Butte Business College, being one of its first students, and landed a job in Virginia City in a bank. In 1892, he became the manager of the Madison House in Virginia City.

Pollard came to Red Lodge in 1899, his wife, Barbara, following him two years later. They took possession of the 35-room Spofford Hotel in 1902, added 25 rooms and renamed it The Pollard. The new hotel had a spacious lobby, dining room, barroom with card and billiard tables, a well-equipped kitchen and a laundry, with a barber shop and bowling alley in the basement.

The dining room was very high class for its day and was noted for its excellent cuisine. It specialized in broiled lobster, quite a feat for a town of this size. The barroom was in the front of the hotel, and later became the town's post office site. The bar was beautifully carved out of mahogany. Before World War One, there was a free lunch at midnight serving roast beef, cheeses, pickles and fancy breads. Tom & Jerry drinks were served to all.

A load of coal was delivered six days a week from the local mines to feed the large steam-powered boilers. After World War One, an automatic Iron Fireman Stoker was installed and later the boiler was converted to gas.

Twenty-five people worked in the hotel in its most prosperous years including a head chef, second cook, kitchen workers, housekeepers and maids, laundry girls, bartenders, waitresses and a porter. When telephone service came to Red Lodge in 1903 the hotel got number "1" and kept the number for quite a few years. The story goes that when the Bell people were making arrangements for their installations, one of their "higher up" men got into trouble one night and wound up in jail. Mr. Pollard bailed him out and the man was so grateful he made sure the hotel had telephone number "1."

The hotel became the gathering place for people from all walks of life when they came to Red Lodge from prospectors, salesmen, gamblers, actors and area ranchers. Many famous people also stayed in the hotel including Gen. Nelson Miles, William

Jennings Bryan, W.A. Clark and Marcus Daly, the Butte "Copper Kings," Jeremiah "Liver Eatin" Johnson, the noted Indian scout, Calamity Jane and Buffalo Bill.

In the late 1890s the Carbon County Bank was located in the corner of the hotel building. A famous personality visited the bank to withdraw some funds, but he did it was a gun. The bank robber was Harry Longworth, known as the Sundance Kid, who surprised the guests at the hotel. He was caught, but later escaped. There is also a story among the "locals" that Ernest Hemingway stayed at the hotel and actually wrote one or two of his stories there. No definite proof of this has ever surfaced.

Thomas Pollard, who became very involved in local civic affairs and politics died in 1942 and his wife sold the hotel in 1946. After the sale it had

various names, among them The Chief, The Tyler and The Cielo Grande, which had plans for a swimming pool, a miniature golf course and many more rooms. This grand idea never materialized. The hotel fell into a long period of decline but in 1991, the Hotel Company of Red Lodge purchased the building. For a year the interior rooms were dismantled and all the windows, ceilings, carpets, furniture, draperies and linens were replaced. The exterior rooms were the first to be completed, and an exercise room and ski storage area were added on the lower floor. Starting in 1992, major renovations on the interior of the building began. The rear gallery was created, the interior rooms expanded and the History Room installed. Office space and a barber shop were remodeled into the dining room and kitchen. Part of the original lobby was kept and remodeled. On June 15, 1994, the newly redone hotel was reopened. Today one can relax in the History Room, or in front of the fireplace in the Gallery or work out in the fully equipped Health Club with exercise equipment, racquet-ball courts and a hot tub and saunas. One can eat in Arthur's Grill well-known throughout the region. Thirty-nine rooms beckon the visitor to Red Lodge which is the eastern gateway for the Beartooth Highway and a major summer and winter recreation region.

The south side entrance of the Spofford Hotel, Dec. 13, 1896. CARBON COUNTY HISTORICAL SOCIETY, TOLMAN COLLECTION

An artist's rendering of the hotel from *The Northwest Magazine*, August 1892. The ornate top story was not built as pictured.

Pollard Hotel waitresses about 1912. CARBON COUNTY HISTORICAL SOCIETY

The Spofford (Pollard) in 1896 showing "Buffalo Bill's" party in front. Notice the facade changes and enlargement of the building in the bottom photo. The Carbon County Bank occupied a corner of the hotel at this time. CARBON COUNTY HISTORICAL SOCIETY, TOLMAN COLLECTION

A 1930s view of the hotel showing J.C. Penney Company and the U.S. Post Office occupying the bottom floor. CARBON COUNTY HISTORICAL SOCIETY

POTOSI HOT SPRINGS

PONY

POTOSI HOT SPRINGS RESORT
BOX 269
PONY, MT 59747
1-406-685-3330
1-888-685-1695
POTOSI@POTOSIRESORT.COM
WWW.POTOSIRESORT.COM
FOUR CABINS WITH FOOD SERVICE
TWO NATURAL HOT SPRINGS POOLS

The area where Potosi Hot Springs Resort is located has a wild history. There are tipi rings in the area–evidence that this area was originally occupied at times by Native American tribes. There is possible evidence that these mountains were even mined as far back as the 1600s by Spanish explorers. However, the current history of Potosi dates back to the late 1800s when the area was developing as a gold mining hot bed. Virginia City was the capital of the state at that time, and Butte was the biggest city in the state. Pony had a population of about 2-4,000 people in those days, whereas today, there are only about 75 year-round residents. It was at this time that President Taft signed the Placer Mining Claims that currently make up the property of Potosi Hot Springs Resort.

This 75-acre holding in the Beaverhead National Forest was set off primarily to become a resort with the focus being the hot springs. Originally, there was a 14-room lodge built in the 1880s on the same site as the current Main Lodge. This beautiful old hotel and restaurant was accessed by cart and buggy only. The owner would drive down the 6.5 mile dirt road and pick up guests at the train line which spurred off

from Harrison and came into Pony. This remote lodge prospered for a number of years until it was sold off to a local rancher in the '30s or 40s, who moved the structure to his ranch. The building was later sold off for lumber. From the day the hotel was removed, the area became a public place for camping, picnicking and enjoying the hot spring fed pool that had been built in 1892. The area remained this way until the 1960s.

At some point the canyon became the home to a

The Cliff Pool as it looks today. PAOLO MARCHESI PHOTO

- 89 -

Resort owners Nick Kern and Christine Stark.

"hippie commune." They apparently moved in and settled in the canyon past the springs. The locals felt they had lost their spot, and in order to get the group to leave, blew up the walls of the pool with dynamite. Needless to say, it worked and the commune left.

In the mid-70s, Pete and Virginia Gross purchased the property and built a residence that is currently the Main Lodge. They lived here for about 10 years as they built another hot spring and rebuilt the walls to the pool (the floor of the pool is still the original floor poured in 1892). They eventually sold the property to Dale and Patty Trapp who lived in the residence for four years before deciding to build four cabins and make a business out of it. The cabins are very well constructed and obviously they put alot of effort into building and furnishing them.

On April 7, 2000, Nick Kern and Christine Stark became the new owners of the resort. Since the purchase, they have made a number of improvements on the property including new hot springs, a new sauna, refurnished the cabins, cleaned up the grounds, and a number of other projects. They have also managed to build a strong, steady business which has gained national media attention as well as a fantastic "word of mouth" reputation.

Hot water seems to flow out of the ground everywhere at Potosi Hot Springs Resort, and is one of the aspects which makes Potosi such a truly unique destination. They currently offer two developed natural hot springs pools. The Cliff Pool, which is 20' by 50' built right into the base of a moss covered granite cliff wall, maintains a year-round temperature of about 90-94 degrees. Located a few feet away from The Cliff Pool is the new wood-fired Finnish sauna house. This recent addition to Potosi, with fantastic views out its multiple windows and beautiful French doors, perfectly complements The Cliff Pool, making it the perfect cool down from the heat of the sauna, especially in the winter.

The Upper Spring at Potosi is a river rock and granite soaking tub enclosed by a pine cabana house with stained glass window. Potosi Creek runs right by the big pane windows. This tub's 102-104 degree

The old lodge.

water is the perfect temperature for hours of soaking pleasure, and with its private use designation each of Potosi's guests get to enjoy this hot spring as their own private piece of paradise.

Just like their natural setting, the water flowing through these pools is as pure as it gets. The mineral tests on the thermal water at Potosi revealed there is no sulfur in the water, which explains why they have no smell. It also showed they are lacking in almost all hard minerals, not only making the water silky smooth, but very healthy and safe. As a result of this purity and the impressive flow-through rates, these pools require no chemicals for treatment or cleaning.

Potosi Hot Springs Resort has four hand-hewn log cabins. Each 700-square-foot cabin can sleep up to six people with a queen bed in the master loft, a queen size sofa bed in the living area, and two European twin beds, all beautifully appointed with fine linens and down comforters. The cabins have fully equipped kitchens, roomy bathrooms, and a romantic river rock fireplace in the living area. Furnishings include overstuffed sofas and chairs, and the western decor in each cabin is based on local wildlife.

The Cliff Pool
before renovation.

QUINN'S HOT SPRINGS RESORT

PARADISE

Quinn's Hot Springs Resort on Highway 135 between St. Regis and Plains in Sanders County is a newly remodeled resort with historic roots. Its history goes clear back to the 1880s when namesake Martin Quinn, a gold prospector, found the springs while following Indian trails. He homesteaded the site, which one had to either hike down to from a steep trail or float down to on the Clark Fork River. About 1885, he built a commercial bathhouse and visitors started to arrive.

At first Quinn would bring his guests from the train stop at Paradise, but by 1910, a railroad line had been laid through the Clark Fork River Canyon and he built a suspension bridge across the river for easy access to his resort. He built the first hotel in 1905 and his business flourished through the end of World War One.

Quinn had met his wife, Fanny Rhodes, a cousin of Rhodesia's founder, Cecil Rhodes, in Helena, where she was cooking at a resort. Fanny fell ill in the Great Influenza epidemic in 1919 and died. Martin Quinn left his resort afterward and went to Texas and entered the oil business. He returned to Montana in 1922 but died of a stroke at his resort in 1932.

His daughter, Minnie Harwood, had six children and two of them, Jack and Dick, decided to revive the resort after returning from service after World War Two. They built the Harwood House Lodge in 1948, which still serves the resort as the Harwood House Restaurant, Quinn's Tavern & Gaming Casino, Fannie's Store & Gift Shop, changing rooms and offices.

A row of cabins was built in the 1940s using lumber from abandoned Civilian Conservation Corps camps. A new row of more modern cabins was built in 2001.

Tourist trends changed in the 1950s and eventually the railroad discontinued passenger travel and the resort fell on hard times. It went through several owners until Dutch-born Andre Meleif of Bozeman bought it in 1998. He has built six new pools, each a different temperature, from 80 degrees in the long lap pool to a hot 105 degrees. In addition, he opened a beautiful rustic mountain lodge on the site of Quinn's family home. In all there are 23 historic and new cabins for rent, along with 15 rooms in the lodge. None of the lodgings have television or telephones to give guests a relaxing visit.

According to general manager, Denise Moreth, the resort has become increasingly popular with guests from Spokane, Idaho and western Montana and more improvements are on the horizon.

Historic cabins
from the 1940s.

The pool area.

Canyon Cabins.

Glacier Lodge.

Sacajawea Hotel

Three Forks

SACAJAWEA HOTEL
5 NORTH MAIN STREET, BOX 648
THREE FORKS, MT 59752
1-406-285-6515
1-888-SACAJAWEA
SACAJAWEAHOTEL@SACAJAWEAHOTEL.COM
WWW.SACAJAWEAHOTEL.COM
31 ROOOMS
RESTAURANT AND BAR
GROUP FACILITIES

Another large railroad-constructed hotel still sits proudly at the north end of Three Forks in Gallatin County. The Sacajawea Hotel was built in 1910 by the Milwaukee Road's purchasing agent John Q. Adams, to serve passengers and crew of the railroad. Three Forks was the jumping-off point for touring Yellowstone Park in the 1910s and '20s.

The hotel was named for Sacajawea, the Shoshone guide woman who accompanied Lewis and Clark on their exploration of the area in 1805. She was captured as a young girl by the Hidatsa tribe and married one of their men, who later lost her in a bet to Charbonneau, the French explorer/trapper.

Sacajawea's knowledge of the area and of native peoples saved the Lewis and Clark group many times. After tracing the Missouri to its roots, the Corps of Discovery needed horses for the portage across the Continental Divide. By a strange turn of luck, Sacajawea was related to the chief of the Shoshone Indians whose summer camp was across the Lemhi pass southwest of Three Forks, and who subsequently aided the group across. She was the only teenager, the only woman and the only Indian in a group of intrepid men and she was invaluable. Had it not been for Sacajawea, the history of this country could have been different.

The hotel is situated across the street from the old Milwaukee depot. Three Forks is in the "Montana Banana Belt," sheltered from extremely bad weather by the Continental Divide. It has more than 300 sunny days per year, little snowfall and reasonably mild temperatures.

The plans for the hotel were drawn by Bozeman architect Fred Willson. The bulk of the hotel was built around the old "Madison House," originally built in 1882 near the confluence of the Jefferson, Madison and Gallatin rivers. The building was rolled on logs to the new site by horse teams from the first location of Three Forks, known as "Old Town." As the story goes, construction was delayed when the contractor lost his horse teams in a poker game. The "Madison House" was split in two and forms the two wings, the dining room and office space at opposite ends of the hotel. The main structure was built in 1910.

The Sac has endured its share of economic misfortune. In 1927, the Milwaukee Railroad extended the line to Gallatin Gateway. The town of Gallatin Gateway then became the final whistle stop

The lobby, at left, has been restored to its early 1900s elegance. Below: the original 100-year-old bar was built out of reclaimed trestle wood. The restaurant is a well-known steakhouse.

for tourists visiting the Park, and the Sacajawea lost much of its business. The tumultuous relationship between the Sacajawea and the Milwaukee Railroad finally ended in 1980 when the historic Three Forks tracks were pulled up.

The first operators of the hotel were Mr. and Mrs. N. Kleber, but a succession of owners followed, the hotel changed hands six times in 80 years. The hotel was owned for nearly 30 years by a brother and sister. In 1991, Smith and Jane Roedel purchased the hotel. They performed extensive renovations drawn up by architect Clark Llewellyn of Three Forks.

The third floor of the hotel was originally a rail worker's dormitory with two baths serving the entire floor. However, in 1991, nine gracious guest rooms (each with a private bath) including an Anniversary Suite, were built. The renovation took eight months to complete.

The Lewis and Clark room in the basement, which housed a barroom and room for drummers to peddle their wares, was also transformed in 1991 into a spacious and comfortable conference facility for groups up to 75. Great care was taken throughout the renovation to preserve the character of the building. Most of the original trim woodwork was refinished, and new sections painstakingly sawed and stained to match the originals. The light fixtures in the lobby are all original, as are the steam heat radiators and the dark spruce beams in the 14-foot ceilings.

The original heating system consisted of two boilers from steam locomotives. The boilers have been replaced with a modern electric heating system, but the boiler stack and steam radiators are still in place in the hotel. The lobby is conspicuously without a fireplace because when the hotel was built its cutting-edge heating technology made wood heat obsolete.

The hotel went through another renovation under the direction of Brian Ryder for Paul Tripp, who purchased the hotel in October of 1998 from the Roedels.

The lobby, dining room and board room now have more than 600 pieces of period inlaid wall paper. The blocky Arts and Craft period lobby paper was a reaction to the florid Victorian decor of the 1800s. The lobby furniture is all new and in keeping with the classic theme. The stoic buck greeting people as they come through the front entrance is more than 70 years old.

The new bar room replaced an outdoor patio between the kitchen and the lobby. The bar itself is reclaimed trestle wood that is more than 100 years old and was once part of a bridge that spanned the Great Salt Lake. A portrait of Sacajawea hangs over the fireplace.

The elegant dining room seats 56 with an adjacent boardroom seating 14. The boardroom is often full of group meetings during the day and at night is available for larger dinner groups, and a complimentary continental breakfast is served there in the morning.

The rocking chairs on the front porch, a Sacajawea Hotel trademark, are not part of the original decor, but they are a great place to put up your feet and rock as the sun sets on the historic Three Forks veranda of the famous old Sacajawea Hotel.

Thirty-three rooms brimming with old-fashioned character replicate the past with lofty ceilings, original turn-of-the-century light fixtures, muted color combinations and antique-inspired furnishings.

In 2001 the owners announced plans to turn the historic hotel into an assisted-living center for senior citizens. The citizens of Three Forks protested to save the hotel and a group of 32 investors called Four Mountains LLC came to the rescue in 2002. They now operate the hotel and are working to increase business locally and regionally.

The Three Forks Hotel (Madison House) was built about 1882 in "Old Town" (Three Forks), which was also called Bridgeville. The town was a stage stop enroute to Virginia City, Bozeman and Helena. GALLATIN COUNTY HISTORICAL SOCIETY, 90.401 P339N

The front part of the Madison House was skidded on logs to its present site and forms one of the hotel's wings today. GALLATIN COUNTY HISTORICAL SOCIETY, P350N

The back of the hotel showing the two wings from the Madison House just before completion of the hotel in 1910.
GALLATIN COUNTY HISTORICAL SOCIETY, P351N

The Sacajawea Hotel after completion in 1910. GALLATIN COUNTY HISTORICAL SOCIETY, P10935

The hotel in the 1940s.

STAGE COACH INN

WEST YELLOWSTONE

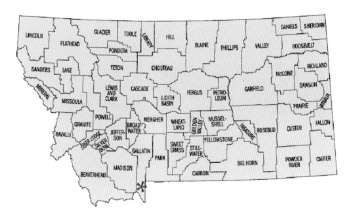

STAGE COACH INN
BOX 160
209 MADISON AVENUE
WEST YELLOWSTONE, MT 59758
1-406-646-7381
1-800-842-2882
91 ROOMS
RESTAURANT AND LOUNGE
GROUP FACILITIES
HOT TUBS AND SAUNA, UNDERGROUND PARKING

The Stage Coach Inn takes up most of the corner of Madison Avenue and Dunraven Street, extending to Electric Street to the west in the tourist town of West Yellowstone. The town is the west entrance to Yellowstone National Park and the town grew up around the branch line of the Oregon Short Line Railroad that reached the west boundary of the park in 1907. On June 11, 1908, the first tourist train arrived.

A post office was established called Riverside and in 1909, the name was changed to Yellowstone with a final change to West Yellowstone in 1920. As more and more tourists arrived at the small settlement by train and later by automobile, a townsite was platted. In 1920, the town was removed from inside the Gallatin National Forest boundary. Tourist facilities sprung up and today the town is a major destination for both summer and winter activities in and around the park in Wyoming, Idaho and Montana.

In 1946, Mr. JL Grimmett of Idaho Falls began construction of the inn which was completed in 1948. It was built in a unique "Western Swiss" chalet design using stone and brick with a dormered exterior. The lobby features a handcrafted, sweeping central staircase carved from Western pine. In the 1950s, a man known as "Doc" Bayless purchased the inn and ran an illicit gambling operation in the basement, complete with wired doors to warn gamblers of trouble. During construction of the Barrel Bar in the 1960s, 47 slot machines were found behind a false wall in the basement.

In 1964, Howard Kelsey and partners purchased the inn for $250,000 and closed it for renovation. The "new" inn celebrated its grand opening in conjunction with the opening of the West Yellowstone Airport in June 1965. Third floor rooms, a new dining room and the Barrel Bar were added.

After operating the inn for many years, Kelsey sold the property to two brothers who operated it for a short time before leaving town. At a court sale in 1981, the inn was purchased by a group of partners including Larry Grimmett, son of the original owner. A spa area with sauna and hot tubs was added during the mid-1980s. In the spring of 1988, the Stage Coach Inn was purchased by its present owner, Ventures West, Inc.

Ventures West began an expansion of the building to add 55 deluxe rooms, a gift shop and underground parking. Construction carefully designed to match the original exterior was completed for a winter opening in January 1990. These deluxe rooms feature custom decor with western motif especially designed for the hotel. The "Historic Wing" of the hotel was remodeled in 1995 to include new wall covers mixed with white pine paneling along with customized wildlife lighting fixtures in the hallways. The natural, old western look was kept intact to keep the heritage of the hotel alive.

STEVI HOTEL

STEVENSVILLE

STEVI HOTEL
107 EAST THIRD STREET
STEVENSVILLE, MT 59870
1-406-777-3087
1-406-550-2007
12 ROOMS

The Stevi Hotel in Stevensville, Ravalli County, started out as a state-of-the-art hospital, one of the most unusual hotel conversions in the state.

W.R. Rodgers built this Classical Revival-style brick and concrete building in 1910 for Dr. William Thornton. It was the only real hospital in the Bitterroot Valley at the time. The building has three stories with Tuscan columns holding up a wide wrap-around veranda. Surgery took place on the second floor and 17 rooms of the second and third floors held patients. Dr. Thornton had his office and residence on the first floor.

In 1917, Dr. Thornton moved his practice to Missoula and Dr. P.S. Rennick assumed ownership of the hospital. He remodeled the building in 1928, enlarging the sun porch and altering the third floor dormers. After Dr. Rennick died in 1939, the hospital closed and for many years the building was a nursing home and later a day-care center.

Kirk and Yvette Slock, originally from Oregon, saw an opportunity in 1999 to take the now empty building and convert it into a homey hotel to serve the small town of Stevensville, which had not had a real hotel for many years. Kirk is in the painting business and after repainting the entire interior, Yvette used her imagination to furnish the 12 rooms with some period decor. Only one room has a private bath but all rooms on the first and second floors have easy access to full bathrooms. The rooms range from full queen-sized beds to small single beds and the quaint lobby area has seen numerous wedding ceremonies. Most of the guests stay for the weddings or for visits to friends and relatives in the area.

Yvette has tried to keep the hotel as authentic as possible and the hotel is worth a stop when traveling through the Bitterroot Valley.

The current hotel has had some facade changes from the original hospital building at right.

Yogo Inn

Lewistown

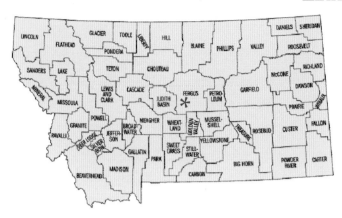

You could call the Yogo Inn in Lewistown, Fergus County, a railroad hotel, sort of. It incorporates the old Mikwaukee Road's station constructed in 1910, but was opened as a hotel in 1962 by the Lewistown Community Hotel Committee. In 1958, two serious fires had burned the Fergus and Burke hotels in Lewistown. People in town began to discuss the need for a large in-town hotel and a committee was formed to raise capital for construction.

On June 11, 1959, it was announced that the community had subscribed $526,000. Construction began and a grand opening was held on Aug. 3, 1962. The hotel opened with 60 rooms, a ballroom, dining room, coffee shop, private dining rooms, cocktail lounge and an indoor pool. Additional construction occurred through the years and it is now the social center for Lewistown with 120 rooms and large group facilities.

The Inn also has the distinction of sitting on the exact site of the geographic center of Montana.

While constructing a large recreation and meeting room in the new addition, workmen found a gold pan and under it a large rock covering a document, dated Feb. 29, 1912. It was set there by pioneer surveyor Will Strafford, who determined the site was the exact center of the state at the time. The facility is now named The Centermark. The exact center of Montana has now been determined by the U.S. Geodetic Survey to be about seven miles northwest of Lewistown.

The 1910 Milwaukee Railroad depot. In 1956 the railroad ceased passenger operations and the depot sat empty.

The front archway of the Inn.

ALL PHOTOS COURTESY YOGO INN.

The Lewistown Community Hotel Company decided in 1961 to demolish the existing depot, with the intent of building everything brand new. As it turned out, it was decided to keep the original depot and build around it. The kitchen of the Inn is the original kitchen which was a part of the depot. The Sapphire Ballroom was once the depot's waiting room area. The guest rooms above the ballroom served as apartments for train conductors.

The lobby area.

CHARLIE RUSSELL CHEW CHOO DINNER TRAIN

Since the Yogo Inn incorporates the former Lewistown Milwaukee Railroad depot, it is fitting that the popular Charlie Russell Chew Choo Dinner Train should be headquartered at the Inn. The train runs once every weekend from Memorial Day through the end of September with special trains on Christmas, New Year's Day and Valentine's Day. It is a 56-mile round-trip journey of approximately four hours, crossing three 150-foot-high trestles, passing through a 2,014-foot tunnel constructed in 1912-13, passing by several old towns and enjoying a catered prime rib dinner. The route follows some of the most scenic country in Central Montana and follows the old Milwaukee Railroad line through the landscape that inspired much of the artwork of the turn-of-the-century western artist, Charlie Russell. Booking and information is through the Yogo Inn.

Montana's Grandest:

Historic Hotels

and Resorts

Gone But Not Forgotten

The area that eventually would be turned into a major resort was first settled as far back as 1850. In 1866, the area was purchased by settler Wilson Redding, an ex-Confederate soldier, for $3,000 in gold. Redding had once traveled to the Alhambra region of Spain and so named it. The site is about 12 miles south of Helena, just off Exit 182 of Interstate 15, along the Alhambra Frontage Road south to the Warm Springs Road junction, in Jefferson County

The curative features of the hot springs water had been known for years and were recognized as the highest mineralized in Montana. A constant flow of more than 50,000 gallons per day at a temperature of 134 degrees F supplied the hotel, baths, plunges and bottling works.

Redding built the first hotel in 1866 and 25 years later a large hotel and cottages replaced the old log structure. Butte miners would travel to the springs to get a cure for lead and arsenic poisoning and to get relief for rheumatism and gout. In addition the resort became a gathering spot for the well-heeled families from Helena.

In 1904, Redding's daughter sold the resort to Mr. and Mrs. Mike J. Sullivan, a prominent Butte athlete, and his wife. They expanded the facilities and heavily promoted the health properties of the water, even shipping tank cars of it to Great Falls to be bottled. Eight trains a day brought visitors to the hotel to "take the waters" in the 1920s. There was a large public plunge in the main bathhouse and separate mud, vapor and plunge baths in the hotel. The hotel's restaurant was well-known for its food, especially its chicken dinners.

On the evening of April 24, 1959, a fire completely destroyed the hotel and the *Great Falls Tribune* reported that only a piano and a little beer were saved. The story goes that the cook set the fire on purpose and later a police investigation discovered he had worked at another resort which burned under mysterious circumstances. A nursing home was soon built on the site and only some remnants of the old spring house and concrete slabs up the valley remain of this once popular resort.

Today only some concrete slabs and wooden frame pieces remain from the springs area which is located up the valley from the resort buildings.

View of Alhambra Hot Springs in 1915. Lime kilns can be seen at the left, a few are still in existence. The actual springs were located up the valley from the resort buildings. TAYLOR COLLECTION

TAYLOR COLLECTION

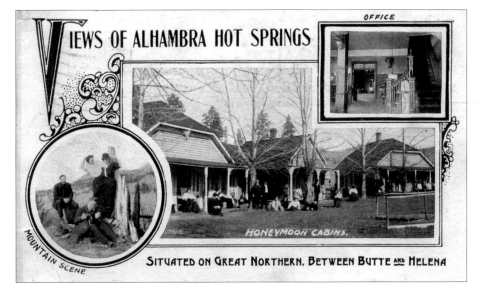

An 1890 view of the entrance to the resort. MHS #940-328

MHS

These two views show an Oddfellows IOOF picnic at Alhambra Hot Springs, no date. MHS #PAC 96-19.7 AND 940-333

Andrus Hotel

The second largest hotel built in Dillon, Beaverhead County, was the Andrus. It was erected by Harry E. Andrus who had recently disposed of his ranching interests in the Sheep Creek Basin. The new building at the corner of Glendale and Idaho streets was built by Jessie M. Warren, a well-known Butte architect, and opened on Feb. 18, 1918. It was constructed of pressed brick and cement and was fireproofed and had an automatic electric elevator. The upper two floors had 65 rooms, 46 of which had private baths. The first floor had five small retail stores, a large tile floor lobby, an office, barber shop, cafe, dining room and kitchen. The total cost was $150,000.

In its day the hotel was very popular with traveling salesmen and visitors from all over the world who passed through Dillon. Before Dillon had a hospital, doctors treated their patients at the hotel. The hotel's bar was not only a popular place but much of Dillon's business was actually settled there. One of the country's most unusual bellboys roamed the halls of the hotel. He was a Great Dane named King Pharoah, who carried bags in his mouth from the train depot to the hotel. Between jobs the dog would sit in one of the big green leather chairs in the lobby.

For over 50 years the business remained in the Andrus family. In 1979, the building was remodeled and opened as a furniture store. The old hotel is still one of the anchor buildings of downtown Dillon even though its glory days as a fine hostelry are long gone.

The Andrus as it looks today. VINOLA SQUIRES PHOTO

The Andrus Hotel at the corner of Idaho and Glendale streets in 1910. BEAVERHEAD COUNTY MUSEUM, 111.11 A-1

A 1951 postcard view of the hotel. The sender circled the rooms they were staying in.

GRAND PUBLIC RECEPTION AND OPENING

—OF THE—

HOTEL ANDRUS

AT DILLON, MONTANA

Thursday Evening, Feb. 14, 1918

From 6 Until 12 o'Clock p. m.

RESERVE YOUR TABLES NOW

Dinner Will Be Served From 6 o'Clock On

Dancing, Music, Feasting, Merry Making

Entertainment by a High Class Troupe of Cabaret Performers

The Hotel will be formally thrown open to the public under the most auspicious circumstances and a cordial invitation is extended to the entire public to inspect Dillon's $150,000.00 Hostlery

BAKER HOTEL

The Baker Hotel was built in 1915 by Frank Grellinger, one of the top railway executives for The Northern Pacific Roadway. He had purchased the land in 1914 from Robert and Margaret Lloyd. This is the second oldest-standing brick structure in the City of Baker, which was founded in 1910.

The hotel was built for people traveling on the Yellowstone Trail (U.S. Highway 12) and also for workers on the railroad. Originally it was for train passengers but, with the decline of passenger trains going through the area in the 1950s, the hotel trade began to suffer. It was later used mainly as a cafe and meeting place during the 1950s through the 1980s, although it did still have rooms for guests.

The contractor of the hotel was a local man by the name of Pratt. He owned property in the area and the name is still commonplace in the town. The architecture and design of the hotel are testament to his craft. The fact that the outside of the building is in good condition some 90 years later also testifies to his craftsmanship.

The hotel was a main focal point for the entire community during this whole time period. Its location on the main street still raised enquiries from passers through the town.

The hotel has also had a history of division within the community. Not long after the hotel was completed the owner founded the Baker Hotel Corporation, but after an argument with other shareholders, the Corporation split and the Gate City Hotel Corporation was founded in 1918. In 1960, it was traded for a ranch just outside of town, deeded to Ruth Saye by Willet Owens.

Most people living in the community still recall the hotel by either working there in their younger years or meeting with people there in the heyday of the '40s and '50s. It has been a popular cornerstone of the community for its entire lifetime.

The Southeastern Montana Area Revitalization Team (SMART) along with the State Historic Preservation Office and The Montana Preservation Alliance are trying to get this building restored for positive use as it has fallen into disrepair and neglect (2004). SMART's phone number is (406) 778-2020.

The building as it looks today.

BIGFORK INN

On a bitterly cold winter day in 1937 a major fire struck Bigfork and changed the town forever–for the better. It was about 5 p.m. on January 7 and the temperature was said to be 20 below zero. The bar in the Bigfork Hotel was filled with patrons, mostly unemployed loggers and traveling salesmen, sipping beer and passing time. Hotel employees kept the wood-fired furnace as hot as possible trying to keep the drafty, wood-framed building warm.

The fire was too hot. Some said an earthquake the summer before may have jarred the chimney out of alignment. A chimney fire started. Soon the wooden building was on fire. Patrons in the bar acted quickly, but not wisely. Some of the contents of the building could have been saved but the patrons decided the most important things to save were the barrels of beer. As the building went up in flames, the barrels were hauled out and promptly froze. "We lost everything but the clothes on our backs," said Kenneth O'Brien, whose parents owned the hotel. "There was no fire department back then. Neighbors brought garden hoses, but the water just froze." O'Brien's parents, Ernie and Catherine, owned the 10-room hotel and the adjoining dance hall. By the time the fire burned out, all they had left were memories and several barrels of frozen beer. And it was January in Montana, in the middle of the Great Depression.

Bigfork had no bank–the State Bank of Bigfork had closed earlier in the Depression. Kalispell was then about a half-days travel and the bankers there had an unwritten rule against loaning more than $1,000 at a time to any Bigfork venture.

O'Brien was a huge man, about six-foot-four and 240 pounds. He ruled the hotel, and some said the town and the school system, by force of personality.

For example, he had a rule that no dirty loggers could come into his dance hall without a bath. When the dirty, tired and lonesome loggers came out of the woods, he'd greet them with a bar of soap and a towel and point them to the hotel's only bathroom. After a bath, they could dance. "He had to be a big man to make loggers bathe," said his son, Edmond O'Brien.

If there were any men of means in Bigfork during the Great Depression who could secure a loan, one of them was Ernie O'Brien. He was a fanatical supporter of President Franklin Delano Roosevelt,

according to his sons.

"He knew how to get jobs," said Edmond. "He had the contacts through the WPA (Works Progress Administration) and people came to him for work and he got it for them. That's how many of the rock walls around Bigfork (including in front of the school) were built.

Ernie O'Brien was the cigar-smoking "mayor of Bigfork," or the "Kingfish" and he was chairman of the school board. He could tell burly loggers to bathe. But still he almost couldn't get a loan to rebuild the hotel.

"He had a hell of a time to get any bank to loan him money," said Kenneth. "He got so discouraged he almost threw in the towel. But then the First National Bank of Kalispell (now Norwest Bank) gave him a loan."

But the "mayor of Bigfork" didn't want to just rebuild the old wooden hotel he had bought in 1914. He had a vision of Bigfork. "He wanted a building that looked like one of the lodges in Glacier Park." He told a newspaper in 1937 that his building would be like a "Swiss Chalet."

Harry Elton, then caretaker of C.J. Kelly Estate on Swan Lake, contracted to build the new hotel, containing 18 rooms, several bathrooms and an apartment for the O'Brien family. Elton was paid $3 a day, the rest of the workers $1 a day.

The log work, still in evidence today, was done mostly by the Fenby brothers of Swan Lake, who also hand-split the cedar shakes that are still on the building. The logs were cut when it was 20 below or more in the Swan, forever trapping frozen sap in the bark.

The miraculous construction job was completed–well, almost completed–by July 4, 1937, less than seven months after the fire. "People wanted to move in so we let them," said Edmond. "They had to walk on planks to get to their rooms, but we let them move in."

The metamorphosis of Bigfork seemed to begin with the building of the new hotel. Gone was the shabby wooden hotel. Arrived was the landmark building that still dominates the architecture of downtown Bigfork.

"Dad could see where the town was going," Edmond said. "The old logging days were over. Bigfork, he always predicted, had a bright future as a resort town." The hotel was always a center of the town's activities. Before the state highway was routed just west of downtown Bigfork, all the highway traffic passed in front of the hotel. It was a popular stop for salesmen and tourists.

Many of the town's schoolteachers and Superintendent of Schools H.A. Veeder were longtime residents of the hotel. Ernie O'Brien, as chairman of the school board, subsidized school salaries by giving free or discounted room and board to school personnel.

The hotel attracted the famous, too. Comedian Red Skelton was a frequent summer guest. Artist Charlie Russell stayed in the hotel as did Virginia Hill, the famous girlfriend of gangster Bugsy Siegel. The O'Brien brothers said Hill's room was used more as a drop-off point for money than as living quarters for Hill.

The hotel, which had its name changed to the Bigfork Inn in 1972, went through several ownerships until 1982. It is now owned and operated as one of the state's most popular restaurants by Bob and Suzie Keenan. Since July 4, 1937, it has been a landmark–or as Edmond O'Brien called it–"the centerpiece of the town."

Two views of the Bigfork Inn a decade apart.

Baxter Hotel

The Baxter has been a fixture in downtown Bozeman, Gallatin County, since it opened in 1929. The Community Hotel Corporation was formed to build the hotel, helping to promote tourism to the area. Eugene Graf, a local entrepreneur, spearheaded the committee. Sixteen prominent businessmen formed the corporation and proposed to sell stock to the public to raise the $200,000 needed for construction. By October 1927, the corporation was $78,000 short of their goal, but their persistence remained and small stock purchases made by the community kept the campaign going. Then a sizable investment of $50,000 was made by George Baxter, a Gallatin County rancher. The board decided to name the hotel in his honor, although many felt it should have been named after Eugene Graf.

Bozeman's leading architect, Fred Willson, designed the building in an Art Deco style. A home was demolished at the northwest corner of Willson and Main to provide the site for construction with additional sites also being purchased. Willson also designed the interior decor, working in the hotel from 1929 to 1951. His intricate work still remains in the building.

On March 29, 1929, the hotel opened under the management of the Roberts-MacNab Hotel Co. They operated the hotel for 20 years and a new 20-year lease was extended to the MacNab brothers. Eugene Graf stayed on as president of the Baxter Hotel Corporation until 1960. The hotel business remained profitable even during the Great Depression but in 1981 a major renovation, scheduled to cost $360,000, took place that turned the hotel rooms into condominiums.

Today the renovated lobby area has five separate food and beverage services: The Pasta Company, the Bacchus Pub, the Garden, the Robin Lounge and the Outback. On the mezzanine is a spacious and versatile ballroom, ideal for seminars, banquets, wedding receptions and dances. Two other rooms can accommodate smaller groups. The Baxter has not lost its historic ambiance or its major place in downtown Bozeman.

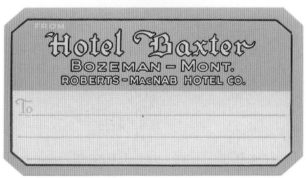

Construction view of the Baxter Hotel Oct. 3, 1928. GALLATIN COUNTY HISTORICAL SOCIETY

The bar in the new Baxter Hotel. The hotel today has five separate food and bar areas: The Pasta Company, the Bacchus Pub, the Garden, the Robin Lounge and the Outback. The Pasta Company offers Italian and Continental cuisine. The Bacchus Pub's decor is a reproduction of a medieval winery in Munich, Germany. The informal Garden is a soup and salad bar. The Robin Lounge offers a comfortable ambience. The Outback features patio dining, weather permitting. GALLATIN COUNTY HISTORICAL SOCIETY

The lobby area has been restored to its original appearance. On the mezzanine is a spacious and versatile ballroom that can be rented out for various group activities. GALLATIN COUNTY HISTORICAL SOCIETY

A large brick building at 307-321 East Main Street in Bozeman was once one of Bozeman's most ambitious building projects, built in hopes the city would become the capital of the new state. George Hancock, an architect from Fargo, North Dakota, established a branch office in Bozeman and over a three-year period designed many local landmarks, including the gothic-styled St. James Episcopal Church (1890-91) and the City High School building (1892).

Hancock's most prominent design was the Hotel Bozeman, financed by the Bozeman Improvement Association for $120,000. The building was completed in 1891. It contained 136 guest rooms, with steam heat and electricity, call bells and fire escapes. A year later an adjoining brick structure to the west, known as the Hotel Bozeman Annex was completed. A temporary footbridge was built from the second floor of the hotel to the second floor of the Opera House so the dancers, staying at the hotel could stroll back and forth without getting muddy. Both buildings were built in a Victorian Commercial style. The hotel was later converted to offices, retail space and apartments.

The Hotel Bozeman building is one of the most impressive in downtown Bozeman. GALLATIN COUNTY HISTORICAL SOCIETY

Notice the facade from this 1890s view of the Hotel Bozeman. GALLATIN COUNTY HISTORICAL SOCIETY

Just south of Four Corners (Highways 191 & 85) west of Bozeman and a few miles north of the Gallatin Gateway Inn is the Bozeman Hot Springs, a new resort built on a very old one.

A local wagon and carriage builder, Jeremiah Mathews, homesteaded the springs area in 1879 and built a 14-foot by 18-foot plunge bath and five bathing rooms. Mathews' Warms Springs water was described as being "remarkably soft, pure and delightfully refreshing for both beverage and bathing purposes," according to the *Bozeman Avant-Courier*.

In 1890, Mathews sold his property to E.M. Ferris for $25,000 and the name was changed to Ferris Hot Springs. Ferris built a two-story hotel and a large plunge and private baths. The *Helena Independent* stated in an April 27, 1890, edition, "There are features and attractions combined with this place that are not to be secured in any other place in the world." Resort guests were brought from Bozeman in horse-drawn coaches and besides the use of the waters they could play lawn tennis and croquet. In 1908, the Gallatin Valley Electric Railway built a 16-mile track from Bozeman to the hot springs and ran trolleys there for years.

An elaborate real estate scheme involved the springs in 1911. A planned subdivision was proposed in land surrounding the resort called Rainbow Land. Grandiose plans were made to sell lots for $150 and to raffle off the hot springs separately. Over 500 tickets were sold and in 1913 a drawing was held and a cattleman from Fort Benton won the resort. The lots were so small that building houses on them was not practical and to this day the subdivision has been a problem with county authorities.

In the early 1920s Sam Collett bought the resort, expanded the facilities and built a maple-floored ballroom on adjacent land. Every weekend during the summers dances were held. By 1931, Georgia Brown was the new owner and poured the pools that are the foundation of the springs today. She added a dance hall and restaurant that entertained visitors from around the country. At the end of the 1930s, the dances declined and attractions changed. Rodeos were held outside and prize fights were held and when the weather was bad the large indoor pool was drained and a boxing ring was set up in it.

Charles Page bought the resort in 1949 after the liquor license had been sold and the dance hall converted to a roller skating rink. A KOA Kampground was added along with 10 rooms on the hot springs building. Page also added the old yellow school bus that was a fixture at the entrance until removed in 2001. He bought more land and tried to interest investors in building a major resort but could not get adequate financing.

Area contractor Dennis Simpson bought the popular resort in 1996 and has remodeled the entire facility including more soaking pools, a dry and wet sauna, juice bar, day care, tanning beds and a large spa and fitness center.

A 1950s view of Bozeman Hot Springs showing the mission-style building and log pool building. GALLATIN COUNTY HISTORICAL SOCIETY

Broadwater Hotel and Natatorium

It is a shame one of the most famous resorts of the West, located just west of Helena, has completely disappeared.

Gold was discovered in the Helena area in July 1864 and the town that grew up around the diggings was boasted as the wealthiest town per capita of its size in the United States. A man named Col. Charles A. Broadwater came to Bannack from his native St. Louis in 1862 and later moved to Helena. He made a fortune in the freighting business and operating trading posts at army posts.

He founded a bank in Helena in 1883 and four short-line railroads in Montana, becoming one of the wealthiest men in Montana and a great booster for the Helena area. In 1888, he hired the prominent Helena architectural firm of Paulson & McConnell to design what would become the world's largest indoor swimming pool. It would be located just east of Helena in an area of known hot springs.

To accompany the pool, known for years as "The Natatorium," he hired the firm of Wallace & Thornbaugh of Helena to design a large hotel. It took over a year for several hundred workers and craftsmen to complete the project which had its grand opening on Aug. 27, 1889 (Montana had become the 41st state in 1889). The Natatorium, with natural hot water, was one of the largest enclosed, pillarless spaces built in the world at the time. It had a huge vaulted roof over a pool 300 feet long and 100 feet wide. At one end a huge twin waterfall poured over a great granite rock structure called the "Cascades." One cascade was natural hot mineral water and the other was pure cold water. The building was built in the Moorish-style with the roof 100 feet high and towers 150 feet high.

The pool was constructed of stone and cement and had a depth from two to 12 feet. It was surrounded by a railed promenade 10 feet in width with 100 steam-heated dressing rooms facing the pool. It was lighted, by day, by 20,000 square feet of colored cathedral glass and electric lamps at night. A million gallons of hot mineral water ran through the pool daily, tempered by cold spring water.

The hotel had two stories with a wrap-around porch, a partial porch on the second story, and a portico underneath the top cupola on the east end of the building. There was a total of about 125 rooms with 10 suites with private baths and fireplaces. Every room was supplied with hot mineral water. Bathrooms were tiled with lavender glass and marble, and all the tubs in the hotel were made of solid porcelain, imported from Europe at a cost of $250 each.

The bridal suite had a bath tub made of solid Italian marble with a quarter inch solid gold inlay strip. Included in the hotel, which was filled with luxurious furnishings, was a ballroom, a kitchen complete with a 10-foot coal range and a walk-in meat cooler, a bakery with a brick oven, a billiard hall, a barber shop, two parlors and an office.

In the dining room were sterling silver chandeliers and lavish velvet carpets covered all parlor,

Today only some trees and an operating fountain remain at the site of the hotel and natatorium. The cupola now stands on a site on the east edge of Helena and can be seen from Interstate 15. Top, the hotel site; bottom, the natatorium site.

hallway and chamber floors. The furniture was upholstered in horsehair, satin and tapestry. There were two plunges with private bathrooms in the hotel itself.

Along with the hotel there was an artificial lake fed by mountain water, horse stables and fountains around the grounds. Electric lamps lighted the garden walks which connected the hotel and Natatorium. Unfortunately the resort, which Colonel Broadwater had invested about $500,000 in, operated at a loss for many years, due in part to the limited population of the Helena area and the entire new state of Montana.

In May 1892, after returning from an Eastern trip, Broadwater had an attack of influenza and died at his hotel. He was 52 years old. His funeral would be the largest ever held in Montana up until that time. After his death, the resort was operated by seven different groups and gradually went into decline, although the Natatorium continued to be very popular.

In the early 1920s, James Breen, who had owned the resort for some years, optioned the resort to the city of Helena with the idea of working with the Northern Pacific Railroad and the Yellowstone Park Hotel and Transportation companies to bring tourists to a rejuvenated Broadwater. There is no record that this idea ever materialized.

Eventually the hotel was turned into a gambling and dance hall and the lower rooms were turned over to gaming tables and slot machines. The longest operator of the resort was the Broadwater Hotel Company which owned it from 1920 to 1939. A California woman paid just $58,000 for the complex and continued to operate the hotel as a gam-

bling concern and supper club until a statewide crackdown on gambling forced the resort to close for good in 1941. Most of the ornate furnishings had either been sold off or stolen by this time.

The demise of the resort actually started in 1935 when a heavy earthquake hit the Helena area and another one three years later broke the pipes supplying the hot springs water to the pool and damaged the Natatorium itself.

During World War II, the commander of the First Special Service Forces, which was training at nearby Fort Harrison suggested the hotel could be used as a rest and recuperative center for servicemen. But this did not happen and in 1945, it was again suggested the resort be converted to a home for the senile and aged of the state. Unfortunately this did not happen either.

In December 1945, Norman Rogers purchased the entire resort for $25,000 with the idea of reopening it to the public. The superstructure over the Natatorium was torn down in 1946 and Rogers had installed new pipes for the now outdoor pool. He also re-roofed the aging hotel and announced he would reopen no later than July 1, 1949. But due to finances he never reopened and the property was fenced off and used to store heavy mining equipment.

On Sept. 22, 1974, an auction was held to sell off the remaining fixtures of the old hotel. In the subsequent years the building was gradually demolished and the remaining boulders of the Natatorium were hauled away. Today hardly anything is left to denote a major resort was on the site. Only some trees, one small portion of the hotel and a fountain ring remain on the sprawling grounds.

The sprawling Broadwater Hotel and Natatorium was located about three miles west of Helena and was one of the great resorts of the West when it opened in 1889, the same year that Montana was admitted into the Union. MHS, #945-791

A postcard view showing the back of the hotel complex.

THE LARGEST NATURAL HOT WATER PLUNGE IN THE WORLD,
HELENA, MONT.

POSTCARD VIEWS
OF THE
NATATORIUM.

236. Broadwater Natatorium, Helena, Mont.

Broadwater Natatorium,
Helena, Mont.

These three views were taken by prominent photographer F. Jay Haynes a year after the hotel opened for business in 1889. The lobby shows examples of the intricate woodwork used throughout the hotel. The parlor shows typical 1890s interior woodwork and furnishings. Bathrooms were as elegant as in any first-class hotel in its day.

MHS, #H-2313

MHS, #H-2315

MHS, #H-2314

MHS, #1989.106.04

Admit

TO THE
BROADWATER PLUNGE

Good for swimming suit, bathroom privileges, towels, etc., and
access to the building at any time.

Manager.

The fabulous Natatorium building was built
in Moorish architectural style and was the
largest pool structure in the world at the
time. MHS, HAYNES FOUNDATION COLLECTION, #H-2318

At the entrance to the Natatorium a statue of "The Boy
with the Leaking Boot" was placed as a fountain fixture.
The elegant Moorish architecture of the pool structure
can be seen in the background. The statue was placed in
the lobby of the First National Bank in Helena many
years ago. MHS, HAYNES FOUNDATION COLLECTION, #H-2320

The needle bath allowed patrons to be showered
from every direction with water of any desired
temperature. MHS, HAYNES FOUNDATION COLLECTION, H-#2316

During the 1930s the character of the complex changed from a first-class hotel to a bar and gambling house. No longer was the buiding illuminated by colored lights, but by the white glow of neon tubes. MHS, #945-782

The "Cascades," a large granite structure from which both cold and natural hot water issued, was at the far end of the 300-foot long Natatorium. This view is from 1890. MHS, HAYNES FOUNDATION COLLECTION, #H-2322

The great structure that housed the pool was seriously damaged by the 1935 earthquake and torn down in 1946. The "Cascades" can be seen at the end of the debris. MHS, #945-832

The debris of the Natatorium was eventually cleaned up and for years the remains of the "Cascades" was all that could be recognized from the great pool. Now all traces of the structure have been removed. MHS, #945-834

The Modernism of the New West
The Hospitality of the Old West

People From All Over the Treasure State Know the Broadwater for Its Distinctive Western Hospitality. . . . For Here's an Atmosphere of Gaiety and Informality That Makes It a Slice of Old Montana, Itself!

At the Broadwater Bars . . .

No visit to Helena would be complete without a visit to these famous bars, for here, old Montana lives again. The unique old furnishings of the pioneer hotel, the modern hospitality, plus your favorite drinks, bring the pleasant interlude to present-day problems.

Distinctively Different Foods . . .

Prepared by expert chefs, have made the Broadwater famous throughout the land. Sizzling steak dinners, turkey, chicken and ravioli dinners, and tasty sandwiches, will make your visit to this famous night club a most enjoyable one.

PLAYING EVERY NIGHT

"MAL" DUKE and His Royal HAWAIIANS

DIRECT FROM SACRAMENTO, CALIF., AND STATION KFBK

PRESENTING
Entertaining Dance Music Styled in
HULA RHYTHMS

For Reservations . . . Phone 1818

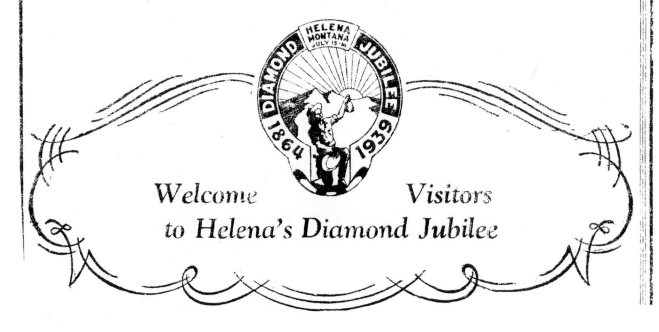

Welcome   *Visitors*
to Helena's Diamond Jubilee

At the corner of Willow Creek Road and the Eastside Highway in the small Bitterroot Valley town of Corvallis is a beautiful Queen Anne home known as the Brooks Hotel.

Before it was a hotel, the home was an architectural drawing and kit advertised in the pages of a mail order catalog. Design No. 37 from a Knoxville, Tennessee, architect cost a builder, $4,535 in 1893. George Dougherty, employed by the Montana Mercantile Company, ordered the house and completed it in 1894. He had previously prepared the housesite by planting shade trees a few years before actual construction (these huge trees, somewhat diminished by age, still frame the house today).

The house has had a few owners through the years. Dougherty moved to Couer d'Alene, Idaho, in 1902, selling the house to Thomas Hefling. He soon left Corvallis as well, moving to Helena to serve as deputy State Treasurer and subsequently rented the house to two families. In 1914, the Brooks family rented then bought the house in 1916 for $4,000, including five acres of bearing orchards, barns, a washroom and ice house.

Louis Brooks was employed as a local mail carrier. He would travel to Woodside twice each day to meet the trains and carry mail back to Corvallis. Often passengers from the train would ask Mr. Brooks to give them a ride to Corvallis along with the mail. From these requests he started his own business of a transfer station from Woodside to Corvallis. With salesmen and travelers looking for food and lodging, Brooks turned his home into a hotel.

In the early years, the hotel served as home to many Corvallis school teachers. Many young men from the area came to court the teachers. Everyone ate together family-style and the day's events, politics and most anything was open to discussion. The Sunday dinners put on by the Brooks family made the hotel well-known up and down the valley. The dinners cost from $1.00 to $1.50 for all you could eat.

Cake mix mogul Duncan Hines stayed at the hotel and Mike and Maureen Mansfield often stayed there. Through the years the hotel received regional and some national attention, including a *Ford Times* article in 1958. The Brooks family continued to operate as a hotel and boarding house until selling out in 1994.

The hotel then became a carpet and vinyl store until Bunny Robbins of Hamilton bought it in the late 1990s and turned it into a delightful year-round Christmas store. The interior of the two-and-one-half story house has been faithfully restored. A large porch had been added to the back of the house in 1917 along with a remodeled kitchen (since greatly upgraded) but the basic house remains unaltered since its construction. The original woodworking and stained glass remain in excellent condition.

Although Corvallis and the valley have grown considerably since the 1890s, the Brooks Hotel remains as a lasting vestige of a bygone era.

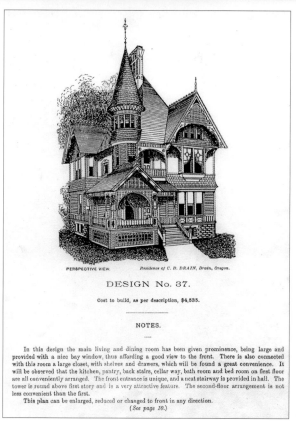

PERSPECTIVE VIEW.   *Residence of C. D. DRAIN, Drain, Oregon.*

DESIGN No. 37.

Cost to build, as per description, $4,535.

NOTES.
—

In this design the main living and dining room has been given prominence, being large and provided with a nice bay window, thus affording a good view to the front. There is also connected with this room a large closet, with shelves and drawers, which will be found a great convenience. It will be observed that the kitchen, pantry, back stairs, cellar way, bath room and bed room on first floor are all conveniently arranged. The front entrance is unique, and a neat stairway is provided in hall. The tower is round above first story and is a very attractive feature. The second-floor arrangement is not less convenient than the first.

This plan can be enlarged, reduced or changed to front in any direction.
(*See page 10.*)

BUTTE HOTELS

At one time Butte was the mining center of the country and with the number of miners working in the area, hotels and boarding houses were springing up everywhere. In addition, the city was the business center of the state and salesmen from every direction came to town to sell their wares. Dozens of hotels sprung up and several buildings are still standing in the uptown area.

The St. James Hotel at 634 Utah Avenue in 1900.
UM#76287, MISSOULA FIRE DEPARTMENT COLLECTION

The old Leonard Hotel on West Granite was built next to W.R. Clark's mansion. It was converted to apartments many years ago. ROD HOCHHALTER PHOTO

Thornton Hotel

One of Butte's most substantial uptown buildings is the Thornton Block at 103 North Wyoming. It was built in 1901 and offered 100 rooms, an elegant ballroom and a bowling alley. In 1906 a northside building was added. The same year the hotel opened a major scandal occurred in one of the rooms. Judge Edward Harney told the press Charlie Clark and two other agents of the Amalgamated Copper Company cornered him in a room and tried to bribe him. Two years later, President Theodore Roosevelt dined at the hotel after giving a speech at the Finlen Hotel across the street. Mayor Pat Mullins ordered the curtains of the restaurant drawn so the public could watch the President eat his dinner. Elmer Johnson,

known by his nickname, "Lemons," worked at the Thornton and was a fixture in Uptown Butte for years. He would deliver carry-out meals in a slow, shuffling gait that was known as "Lemon's stride," all the while balancing a food tray on his head. The Anaconda Company bought the building in 1947 and used is as an employee recreation center and private club.

The Thornton in the 1920s.

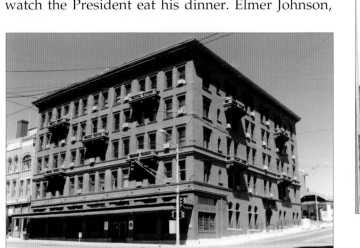

Leggat Hotel

The Butte Opera House occupied the present site of the Leggat Hotel at 50 West Broadway. The Opera House was destroyed by fire on July 23, 1888, and then rebuilt. It was later known as the Empress Theater and it too was destroyed by fire on May 25, 1912. On Jan. 23, 1914 a six-story hotel, the Leggat, opened with 91 rooms. The highest priced rooms were supposedly finished in mahogany, bird's eye maple, oak, walnut or mission oak. The hotel has been closed for years but has about 100 apartment units.

The Park Hotel in the 200 block of West Park was built about 1900. It has been vacant for over 50 years. ROD HOCHHALTER PHOTO

TOWEY HOTEL

The Towey Hotel at 11 South Montana Street was built in 1907 by John Harris for his wife, Elizabeth. It was first called The Harris Block Hotel, with a restaurant in the basement, a bar on the main floor, 30 guest rooms and an apartment for the manager. In 1950 Bessie Towey bought and ran the hotel with a bookstore on the main floor. Today the building has updated plumbing and wiring and serves as an antique mall on the main floor for owners, Jackie and Robert Rolison. It no longer serves as a hotel.

The Lincoln Hotel also in the 200 block of West Park was built about 1910 and has been converted into apartments. ROD HOCHHALTER PHOTO

THE CADILLAC

The original Cadillac Hotel was a three-story, wooden building erected in 1907 on Central Avenue in Whitefish, Flathead County. The town became a major division point for the Great Northern Railroad in 1904. In 1910, the famous temperance lady, Carrie Nation made a visit to Whitefish. A delegation of local W.C.T.U. ladies met her at the train station and took her to the Cadillac Hotel for her overnight stay. When she found out the hotel also had an attached saloon, she refused to stay there and was taken to the Methodist parsonage. She proceeded to lecture bar owners and patrons on the evils of "drink" and got into several minor altercations with some of the townspeople and a railroad employee before leaving town. In 1922, the New Cadillac Hotel was built next door to the old hotel. It was remodeled in 1971 and torn down in 1994 to make way for the Black Star Brewery building. The old hotel was converted to the Hanging Tree Lounge and was a popular establishment for locals and tourists. The lounge was named for well-known western author and Whitefish native Dorothy Johnson's short story, "The Hang-

ing Tree," which was made into a major motion picture. The original hotel was eventually torn down and a Mexican restaurant was built in its place.

The new Cadillac Hotel in the 1920s.

STUMPTOWN HISTORICAL SOCIETY PHOTOS.

The hotel after the 1971 remodel. The original hotel is gone, replaced with a Mexican restaurant.

Corwin Hot Springs

In 1902, Julius LaDuke claimed a hot springs site just south of the future resort of Corwin Springs. He built a small plunge and boarding house. Access to LaDuke Springs was by a rough road between Livingston and Gardiner and then, first by ferry across the Yellowstone River, and later, by a suspension bridge. LaDuke's four-year-old son fell into the hot springs and was scalded to death in 1905 as the water comes out of the ground at 154 degrees F.

Dr. Frank E. Corwin was the resident physician at nearby Chico Hot Springs from 1902 to 1908 when he left to help establish the resort that would bear his name. He resided at Corwin until 1912 when he moved to Hunters Hot Springs near Springdale, also in Park County.

In 1908, a group of Montana entrepreneurs led by Livingston banker Charles Hefferlin, Clyde Park area rancher, John Holliday and local dude ranch owner James Norris "Dick" Randall formed the Electric Hot Springs Company to construct a hotel and hot springs natatorium seven miles north of Gardiner on the Northern Pacific Railway's Yellowstone Park branch line. Local physician Dr. Frank Corwin fronted the money and the company purchased water rights to the La Duke hot springs two miles to the south. In all the company raised over $100,000 to build the resort.

The Corwin Hot Springs Hotel and Natatorium opened for business in July 1909. The hotel, which was modeled after spa hotels in Europe, offered hot and cold running water, electric lights, steam heat and telephones as well as the mineral hot springs, all for $15 a week. Dr. Corwin helped design the 72-room resort hotel and the plunge. Water for the plunge and hot water for steam heat was piped over two miles from the springs at LaDuke.

A 50-foot by 80-foot plunge was built next to the hotel with the hot water flowing continuously through it, providing a complete change of water every six minutes. In addition, the resort featured tub baths, vapor baths and private plunges.

The resort was on the east side of the Yellowstone River and the railroad right-of-way was on the west side of the river. The county, with funds provided by the resort company, con-

Electric Hot Springs, 1914. MHS, H-6593 HAYNES COLL.

structed a bridge to cross the river to connect the railroad and the resort. A livery barn was built on the property to house the horses, wagons and buggies used to transport patrons to and from the Northern Pacific depot.

Due to the area's small population and the popularity of nearby Chico Hot Springs, the resort ran into financial troubles just six months after opening.

Fire hydrants were installed at the four corners of the hotel to give what was heralded as adequate fire protection. But it wasn't enough as both the hotel and plunge buildings burned to the ground in November 1916.

In the late 1920s, the resort site and water rights along with 20,000 surrounding acres, were purchased by Walter Hill, son of railroad magnate James J. Hill. Hill rebuilt the plunge cabins, a dance hall, restaurant and added a nine-hole golf course to the grounds and operated the complex as the Eagles Nest Dude Ranch. In the subsequent years, several different people owned the site and in the 1940s the resort advertised itself as having "vapor and massage baths for ladies and gentlemen...electric lights, steam heat, hot and cold running water and telephones in all rooms." Local activities were geared toward trap shooting, fishing and horseback riding for men and hair dressing, manicures and shampoos for women.

A 1939 Montana state guidebook stated the resort had cabins, a dance hall, restaurant, golf course, and a concrete plunge. The community of Corwin Springs included a grocery store/post office and school all in proximity to the railroad depot. In the 1940s, the rebuilt resort closed for good although Camp Mustang, owned by Margaret Starkweather, operated at the site in the 1970s.

Elizabeth Claire Prophet's Church Universal & Triumphant (CUT) purchased the property in 1981 and razed the existing buildings, except the original barn. The church developed the site as the Royal Teton Ranch with homes and a mobile home park.

Today all that remains of this elegant resort are parts of the plunge near the old iron bridge, a trace of hotel and possibly a concrete foundation of an old bathhouse at LaDuke Springs.

FORT BENTON HOTELS

CHOTEAU HOUSE

The Choteau House began life as a two-story wood-frame building on Front Street. It was lined with adobe on the insides and had about 15 rooms. Built by two well-known Montana entrepreneurs, T.C. Power and I.G. Baker in 1868, the new hotel was located on the steamboat levee a block and a half from the old fur trading post. It was first named the Thwing House after its proprietor, Mrs. Thwing. Passengers could depart their steamboat, walk across the street and register in one of the best hotels in Montana.

During the 1870s, the Fort Benton Military Post leased the hotel for use as officers' quarters and housed post commander Major Guido Ilges among the officers. In 1879, Jere Sullivan and Harry Hill bought the hotel and reopened it in the spring of 1880 under the name Choteau House. In 1882, Hill sold out and Sullivan continued to operate it as a hotel and social center for the town until his death in 1919.

An adobe building next door was used as a saloon for the hotel and in 1900 the saloon was rebuilt in brick, adding 12 rooms overhead as an annex to the hotel. Three years later, Sullivan replaced the old wooden landmark building with a modern frame, brick veneer hotel, which had 20 rooms and a dining room. A third story and 12 more rooms were added in 1910, the final change. The hotel remained in operation until 1969, perhaps the longest life of any hotel in Montana. The building still stands on Front Street.

CENTENNIAL HOTEL

The wood-framed Centennial Hotel opened for business in 1877, owned by Robert Mills and Robert S. Culbertson. Culbertson was the nephew of Alexander Culbertson, the founder of Fort Benton. The partnership dissolved in 1881, and Culbertson became the full owner. The next year, the old hotel was demolished so that a brick hotel could be constructed.

The new Pacific Hotel, as it was now called, began operations on Sept. 29, 1882. Over the years, the hotel became known as the Culbertson House and operations continued in the family until 1941. The building continued in use as a cafe and Coast-to-Coast Hardware until the late 1980s and is now undergoing restoration.

PHOTOS BY JACK LEPLEY, INFORMATION BY KEN ROBISON

GLADSTONE HOTEL

The small town of Circle is located in McCone County in eastern Montana. It's National Register hotel is called the Gladstone which has sat empty for many years. It opened on Main Street on Dec. 24, 1915. A corporation of Circle, Glendive and Brockway men started the hotel in 1914 in anticipation of homesteaders coming to the area and the prospect of the Great Northern Railroad mainlining through the new town. This did not happen due to World War One but the Northern Pacific Railroad did build a spur to Circle from Glendive in 1928.

The original hotel was a two-story frame building with rooms consisting of a bed and dresser, a wash bowl, a pitcher of water and a "pot." The "pot" became known as the "thunder mug," and never lost its popularity in cold weather. A Delco motor furnished the electricity for the light bulb hanging by a cord from the ceiling. In the early days central electricity for the town was a rare commodity and considered a luxury. There were 24 rooms, a restaurant, a bar on the east side of the building and a bar in the basement.

Many owners operated the hotel through the years. In the early 1950s a 10-unit motel was built adjacent and the original rooms were updated. Although the hotel has been closed and empty for many years, it served the citizens of Circle well during the Great Depression, two World Wars, drought and the up and down economic conditions of eastern Montana.

Main Street, looking west in Circle, 1940s. The Gladstone Hotel and Fountain Cafe are on the right. The hotel today, above, needs some tender loving care.
COURTESY DENNIS AND KAREN WOLFF

Grand Hotel/Hotel General Custer

An elegant hotel in Billings named The Grand was constructed at the corner of First Avenue North and 27th Street in 1885-86 by J.J. Walk and I.I. Nickey. Walk was the first man to bring a herd of cattle to southeastern Montana from Oregon.

The architect for The Grand and its first addition was J.G. Link, who established the first architectural firm in Montana in 1896. A native of Germany, Link studied architecture at the Royal Academy in Bavaria and moved to Denver, Colorado, in 1887. In 1896, he collaborated with J.C. Paulsen, State Architect of Montana, to design the Montana State Capitol. Link was in several different partnerships through the years and in 1930 formed J.G. Link & Company in Billings with his two sons. Many of the outstanding buildings in Montana and surrounding states are the result of Link's vision including courthouses, hospitals, schools, dormitories, hotels (including the Northern in Billings) and the Montana Building for the 1904 St. Louis World's Fair. Link died in 1954.

The Grand was the center of society in early-day Billings with dinner there serving buffalo tongue, guinea hen under glass and vintage wines. In 1896, George F. Benninghoff took over the hotel and, "Uncle George" as he was known, kept up the reputation of the hotel.

In the early 1900s an addition was built on the 27th Street side and in the 1920s, the original part of the building burned but was rebuilt shortly thereafter. In the early 1940s, three additional floors were added and the name was changed to the Hotel General Custer. In 1951 another addition was added. An investment company bought the building in January 1979 and converted it into office space, preserving and restoring some of the ambience of the old Grand Hotel.

The Grand Hotel in the late 1800s before the early 1900s addition.
WESTERN HERITAGE CENTER, BILLINGS

A 1908 postcard showing the addition.

The New Grand in the 1920s after rebuilding from the fire.

The Hotel General Custer in the early 1960s showing the three additional floors built on the old Grand Hotel. WESTERN HERITAGE CENTER, BILLINGS

Graves Hotel

The Graves Hotel was the first large structure rebuilt after the Harlowton fire of 1907, a disaster that almost completely destroyed the business district of the town. The hotel was the center of community life since its opening in 1909 by being a business and social meeting place for all the residents of Wheatland County. It was the first sandstone building erected in town and is a good example of the stone architecture peculiar to the area. The sandstone was quarried out of the cliff upon which the hotel was built and the hotel was constructed by German immigrant August Pollman.

A.C. "Chris" Graves was fondly called the "Father of Harlowton." He gave the new Milwaukee Railroad the land for its depot and shops and placed his hotel on top of "Main Street Hill" (Central Avenue) overlooking the Mussellshell Valley and the railroad yards. Graves died in an auto accident at the young age of 47.

On June 1, 1908, The Graves Hotel Company was organized with a capital stock of $20,000. Originally the hotel was built in an L shape so that as business increased, the building could be squared off and enlarged. It is a three-story structure with a flat roof with metal trim along the roof line. A unique metal cupola on the roof demostrates a Gothic Revival influence. A wooden cornice centrally located on the roof edge of the hotel's eastern exposure bears the words: Graves Hotel–1908. The second floor veranda is surrounded by a four foot high white banister and measures 150 feet along the southern and eastern exposures of the building. The main floor veranda is supported by 14 white doric columns, seven on each exposure, which are set upon a cement porch following the contours of the hilltop lot. Oak was used throughout the interior of the building including the front staircase.

The grand opening of the hotel was held on June 19, 1909. A newspaper reported the event: "It was a proud and happy moment for the promoter, A.C. Graves, and the proprietor, J.N. Kleber. At nine o'clock the guests began to gather at the hotel, which was brilliant in the most elaborate electrical display

in this section of Montana. The building dazzled... The Harlowton Band played special music for the occasion...the lobby and dining room were festooned in colors of the flag... costly bouquets of cut flowers gave a finishing touch. At 9:20, the guests formed a procession in the lobby and spacious hall on the second floor. The orchestra struck up a smart two-step... Mr. and Mrs. A.C. Graves led the Grand March, followed by Mr. and Mrs. Kleber... Dancing was resumed and 'the merry making did not break up until nearly dawn.'"

The hotel has been closed for some years and after a fire in the early 1990s, the building had to be brought up to modern codes. The new owner, Rick Harpel of Tumwater, Washington, has been working to remodel the 42 rooms, lobby and dining room. A bar and cafe have been opened in the building for a few years. The main entrance to the lobby was

originally at the corner under the cupola and it is planned to restore it in the future.

The restoration process is slow due to costs involved and the uncertain economic conditions in this part of Montana, but the Graves Hotel deserves to be brought back to its former elegance.

The Graves Hotel in 1913. COURTESY GERALD MILLER, HARLOWTON

PARK HOTEL

In 1885, Great Falls citizens started to boast the idea of more and larger hotels for the city. There were several new ones, among them; the Cascade, Grand, Pioneer, Dirkug and Park.

The Park was the most prominent, built by Paris Gibson and H.O. Chowen and opened on Sept. 1, 1886, at the corner of Central Avenue and Park Drive in downtown Great Falls. The main entrance was on Central Avenue but women were required to enter from the side street. The original building was two-and-a-half stories high with 25 rooms and apartments, a large dining room, kitchen, barroom and piazzas that encircled the building and enabled a view of the Missouri River. In 1887, the hotel was extended an additional 100 feet on Park Drive and the addition made it a three-story structure with 90 rooms and a 250-foot veranda.

Many prominent Montana men stayed in the hotel on their visits to Great Falls including, "Copper Barons" Marcus Daly, W.A. Clark and F.A. Heinze from Butte, and James J. Hill, builder of the Great Northern Railway. William Jennings Bryan, the "Great Commoner," stayed twice in 1897 and 1907. Senator Robert M. La Follette from Ohio, Crown Prince Albert of Belgium, Mark Twain, Ronald Amundson, William Howard Taft and John Philip Sousa all stayed at the hotel through the years.

Like many other large city hotels, the Park was badly damaged by fire in 1913 and subsequently torn down to build the present building, which was owned by the New Park Hotel Company, a consortium of Great Falls businessmen. It is a large five-story rectangular building with light-colored brick veneer, concrete foundations and decorative terra cotta trim. The roof is built up and the extended terra cotta parapet features shaped, stepped and battlemented corner bays with a tall, open balustrade extending along the north and east roof lines. Two large balconies with terra cotta tile-covered pent roofs are located on the top central north and east walls and supported by brackets. Original plans specified a ballroom, banquet and dining rooms on the first floor and a Turkish bath in the basement.

With the demise of most of the large hotels in downtown areas in the 1970s, the reconstruction of the hotel started in July 1970 to convert the building into efficiency and one-bedroom apartments with rent supplements. The total cost of the project was in excess of $1.1 million and it is now called "The Downtowner Apartments."

The first Park Hotel in 1898 with its third story addition and 250-foot veranda. CASCADE COUNTY HISTORICAL SOCIETY, 87-2

This menu was the first job noted artist Charlie Russell got in Great Falls in 1897. He was paid $25 for making 75 menus for the hotel's Christmas dinner. CASCADE COUNTY HISTORICAL SOCIETY, 97.44.1

Middle left and bottom: the elegant Park Hotel in the 1920s. CASCADE COUNTY HISTORICAL SOCIETY, 227-155

THE RAINBOW

One of Montana's finest city hotels, the Rainbow in Great Falls, was opened in April 1911 by the Great Falls Townsite Co. on 3rd Street North. The 132-room hotel was built for $400,000 with $150,000 worth of improvements in the late 1930s, including installation of a bar and cocktail lounge. When the hotel opened, like the Park in Great Falls, it had some areas off-limits to women including the male smoking room, the Palm Room, where early-day business deals were made.

In 1927, the hotel agreed to allow airships (blimps) to land on its roof, starting in 1928, but apparently this never actually happened.

In 1944, the hotel was sold and the operation was assumed by L.W. Carter, who also managed the Grand (Northern) Hotel in Billings and the La Bonte in Douglas, Wyoming.

During World War Two, hotel guests included both Russian and American military personnel who were stationed at Great Falls for the Lend-Lease Program (aircraft) to Russia. The hotel also hosted many famous guests through the years including Bob Hope, Sonny and Cher, Glen Campbell, Frank "Bring 'Em Back Alive" Buck and Don the Beachcomber. Cowboy star Gene Autry even bought the hotel's ornate back bar in 1956.

Over the years the Rainbow was opened and closed at various times due to financial problems or remodeling. At some point, possibly in the 1950s, the hotel was enlarged and later the facade and roof line were considerably altered to the look of today.

In the 1970s, the hotel was used primarily to house tour groups and fell on hard times. In 1980, the hotel was bought and refurbished to try and bring back its former elegance but it had a hard time making money, even with large low-interest loans. Finally in 1994, Leisure Care Inc. purchased the old hotel from the FDIC and remodeled it into about 90 assisted living apartments. The 4,000-square foot atrium rises three stories surrounded by the new apartments. Verandas, fountains and nighttime lighting add charm to the area which is filled with outdoor café-style wrought iron tables and chairs.

The Rainbow has again become a building in Great Falls that residents can be proud of.

The hotel building today has a new use as apartments for assisted living patrons.

Postcard view of the
dining room, 1930s.

Postcard view of the
lobby, early 1900s.

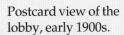

A 1912 postcard view
of the Palm Room.

Early 1900s postcard
view of the hotel.

The Rainbow banquet room in the 1930s. In the back corner is a replica of a Northern Pacific observation car with the "Oriental Limited" sign on the front. CASCADE COUNTY HISTORICAL SOCIETY, 90.26.573

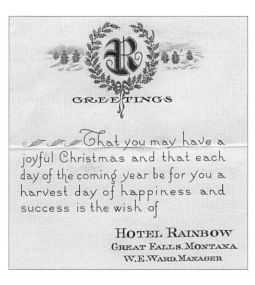

Two views of the Rainbow Hotel in the 1920s (middle) and 1940s (bottom). Notice the different signage and portico alterations from the two decades. Compare these photos with the modern expanded hotel building on page 137. CASCADE COUNTY HISTORICAL SOCIETY, 89.26.208 (MIDDLE) AND 90.26.338 (BOTTOM).

SUMMER IN GIBSON PARK

WATERFOWL ON LAKE IN GIBSON PARK

SKILLET SPECIAL—65c

Tomato Juice
Ham and Eggs, Country Style
American Fried Potatoes
Toast or Hot Rolls
Preserves

Coffee   Tea   Milk

**RAINBOW
SALAD BOWL—75c**

Fresh Lobster Meat
Shredded Lettuce
Tomato Quarters
Hard Boiled Eggs
French or Rainbow Dressing
or
Mayonnaise
Melba Toast or Hot Rolls

Coffee   Tea   Milk

STEAK SANDWICH—45c

Choice
Luncheon Soup or Juice
Steak Sandwich on Toast
French Fried Potatoes

Coffee   Tea   Milk

BRUNCH SPECIAL—60c

Orange Juice
Thick French Toast
Canadian Style Bacon
Currant Jelly or Honey

Coffee   Tea   Milk

HOTEL RAINBOW
LUNCHEON MENU

Choice of

Tomato Juice Cocktail
or
French Onion Soup   Au Gratin
or
Hearts of Lettuce   Rainbow Dressing

▲

Poached Columbia River Salmon   Strip Anchovies ___.75
Hungarian Veal Goulash   Macaroni ___.75
Boiled Brisket of Corned Beef   Green Beans ___.75
Turkey, Mushrooms, Spaghetti and Grated Cheese   en Casserole ___.75
Skillet Dish of Swiss Steak and Bordelaise Sauce ___.60
Crabmeat and Apple Salad   Asparagus   Assorted Cheese ___.65
Rainbow Fruit Salad   Toasted Cheese Sandwiches ___.60
Rice Cakes   Jones Farm Sausage   Maple Syrup ___.50
French Toasted Bacon and Cheese Sandwich   Grape Jelly ___.50
Poached Egg on Creamed Ham and Mushrooms ___.50

▲

Whipped Potatoes   Braised Cabbage

▲

Bon Bon Rolls

▲

DESSERTS

▲

Fresh Apple or Strawberry Rhubarb Pie
Pineapple Delight
Nesselrode Ice Cream or Grape Sherbet

▲

Coffee, Tea or Milk

▲▲

Served From 12 to 2 P. M.
Monday April 14, 1941

(6) **BLUE POINT OYSTERS ON SHELL   COCKTAIL SAUCE** ___.60

Dinner Menu
////

HOT OR COLD CONSOMME
CHICKEN NOODLE SOUP

1. MONTANA MOUNTAIN TROUT SAUTE MENUIERE...$1.50

2. BROILED LOBSTER TAILS SLICED LEMONS...$1.75

3. SHIRRED EGGS WITH PORK TENDERLOIN...$1.25

4. YOUNG CHICKEN DRESSING CURRANT JELLY...$1.50

5. BAKED SUGAR-CURED HAM AU NATURAL...$1.40

6. TOP SIRLOIN STEAK FINANCERE IN SKILLET DISH...$1.50

O'BRIEN AU GRATIN POTATOES   FRESH ASPARAGUS

HOT ROLLS

COMBINATION VEGETABLE SALAD RAINBOW DRESSING

DESSERTS

COCOANUT CREAM PIE

CHOCOLATE PARFAIT   SHERBET

FRUIT JELLO   CUP CUSTARD

ASSORTED CHEESE PLATE BENTS WAFERS

COFFEE, TEA OR MILK

SERVED FROM 5:30 TO 8:00 P.M.
SUNDAY, MARCH 26, 1944

BLUE POINT OYSTERS ON HALF SHELL.....75¢

All Prices Listed Hereon Are at or Below Our Ceiling Prices as of April 4 to 10, 1943

Wartime menu for the Rainbow Hotel dining room.

1980 ad.

RAINBOW HOTEL
"A Carter Operated Hotel"
GREAT FALLS · MONTANA

C. PAT EGAN
RESIDENT MANAGER

The Hardin Hotel

ardin's first hotel, The Hardin, was a two-story white frame building that stood on the corner of Center and Railroad streets. Robert Anderson, one of the earliest residents of the new town, built the hotel in 1907, which was initially named the Anderson Hotel. There were 20 rooms on the second floor while the first floor had a bar, dining room and kitchen. Mr. Anderson was returning from Helena, where he had to appear in court for selling liquor to Indians, when the train he was in collided with another one near Park City, killing 21 people in October 1908.

Mrs. Anderson ran the hotel afterwards and remodeled it as the town was expanding rapidly. She sold it in 1911 to Kate McEvoy who ran it until 1942 when her son and daughter purchased it. They kept it until 1951 when it was sold for $18,000. In the ensuing years, the building deteriorated and the City Council finally demanded the hotel close because of "improperly vented gas heaters, leaks in the roof, and a general need of more cleanliness." There was enough carbon monoxide to "endanger human life." The "Pride of Hardin" finally burned on Aug. 31, 1967.

Being the center of large mining operations and in 1889, the new state capital, Helena became the social and political city of the state. The need for adequate hotel accommodations for the many people visiting Helena became apparent. The first real hotel, The International, was erected in 1869 and later, The Cosmopolitan would become the leading hotel in the entire territory for over 20 years. In the 1880s, other hotels such as the Hotel Helena on Grand Street; the Grand Hotel on Main; the Helena Hotel on Grand Street; and the Merchants Hotel on Broadway, which was the site of the first Montana State Legislative Session in 1890, were built. Other hotels were also built in downtown Helena through the years but today only the Great Norther upholds the traditions of the past.

HOT SPRING HOTEL!

HORACE MATTISON, Proprietor.

The proprietor of this magnificent

HOTEL AND CELEBRATED HOT SPRINGS,

Three miles north of Helena, has, at great expense, re-arranged and refitted the entire premises, so that now

PLEASURE SEEKERS, INVALIDS

And all who wish to spend an hour, a day, or a week, pleasantly and profitably, will find this popular resort the most

Attractive Spot of the Mountain Regions.

THE MOST TASTY AND ATTRACTIVE

Garden!
IN THE TERRITORY.

Every facility is afforded for

BALLS, SOCIAL PARTIES,

Pic Nics, Etc.

In visiting the metropolis do not forget the

HOT SPRINGS.

This ad from the 1868 Helena Business Directory is promoting the first Wassweiler-owned hotel at the site of the 1889 Broadwater Hotel. Apparently a Mr. Horace Mattison was running the property in 1868 but Ferdinand Wassweiler would soon take it back.

HELENA ADVERTISEMENTS.

MADAM COADY

Takes pleasure in announcing to her friends in the Territory, as well as to the

LADIES AND GENTLEMEN OF HELENA,

That she has spared no expense towards making

THE 2 MILE HOUSE

The Favorite Resort of Pleasure Seekers.

This House is distant only 2 miles from Helena on the

Hot Spring Road

She is now prepared to entertain

GUESTS AND PRIVATE PARTIES,

In the most elegant and sumptuous style.

THE TABLE will be, at all times, supplied With the Best the Market affords.

The Bar

Is furnished with the

FINEST LIQUORS AND CHOICEST CIGARS

IN MONTANA.

A No. 1 Circular Race Course,

1 Mile in Length, Adjoins the House.

Horses trained and kept on reasonable terms.

Do not forget in your rides or drives to stop at the

TWO MILE HOUSE,

Apparently this was a separate resort in the Helena area in 1868.

WASSWEILER HOTEL AND BATHHOUSE

Ferdinand and Caroline Wassweiler settled about two miles west of Helena in 1865 on 160 acres. They operated a small hotel and bathhouse near where the famous Broadwater Hotel would later be built. They gained title to the land and two hot water springs near Ten Mile Creek in 1869. The mineral water offered area miners a welcome respite from the dusty gold mining camp at Last Chance Gulch.

In need of cash, the Wassweilers mortgaged half their property for $1,500 in "fine bankable gold dust," paying up in 1872. Again short of funds, the Wassweilers sold their hotel and water rights in 1874 to Col. Charles Broadwater. Broadwater ran the hotel until 1889 when his new hotel and natatorium opened on the property.

Wassweiler built his second hotel on his remaining 80 acres in 1883. The hotel and bathhouse remain today. The walls of the main building are brick resting on fieldstone. Seven exterior doors to separate rooms accommodated hotel guests, and four brick chimneys, venting for woodstoves, pierce the gabled rooflines. The outbuilding of native fieldstone served as the bathhouse with each of four compartments outfitted with wooden tubs. An extension was added sometime later on the east side of the hotel building.

According to the Helena Business Directory of 1868, "The Hot Springs....is destined, at some future day, to be to Montana what Saratoga now is to New York. These springs, both hot and cold, are pronounced by able physicians as possessing medicinal properties of rare virtue. They are at present the resort of invalids, visitor and pleasure seeker. The hotel at the Springs is fitted up in an elegant manner, as also are the grounds. The bathing facilities are good; and, in fact, everything connected with this resort is conducted in the best possible manner. The stranger, visiting Helena, should by all means pay these noted Springs a visit."

The hotel and bathhouse went through several owners and assorted financial problems before finally closing in 1904. Today these buildings, which are used for an antique mall, are the last remainders of the hot springs resort business in the Helena area.

A side view of Wassweiler's second hotel showing some of the seven doors that led into the individual rooms. The later addition is to the right.

The front of the old Wassweiler Hotel with the remains of a wrap around porch. A portion of the old bathhouse can be seen at the right.

Wassweiler's hotel at its original site close to where the Broadwater Hotel would be built. MHS, #951-609

-144-

The Grandon Hotel, formerly at the corner of Sixth and Warren, was built in 1885. The building, built in the Queen Anne-style, first housed the A.R. Gates grocery store. Gates' son, Grandon, was born the year the building was built and the proud father named the block after him. A few years later, Gates decided it would be more profitable to turn the building into a hotel. Later turned into a rooming house for the elderly, it burned down in 1968 with tragic results when several residents died. MHS, #953.546

The old Bristol Hotel, formerly at the corner of Main and State streets, was built in 1887 and was first known as The Penn Block. Then the Woolridge House in 1890 and in 1891, the name was changed to the Bristol when Finlay Urquhart purchased it. During the early years, retail stores occupied the ground floor, but this

later photo shows the hotel on the ground floor. For a period of time the Bristol was the leading hotel in Helena. Around 1916, Mr. and Mrs. Jack Williams bought the building and in 1956, Mr. and Mrs. Bill Bompart bought the hotel and upgraded it considerably. The building to the left was the annex and a portion of an enclosed bridge that crossed high above State Street to the Lissner Baths and Spring Water Emporium can be seen. But the Bristol, like many of Helena's elegant, historic buildings, could not escape the wrecking ball in the name of Urban Renewal. MHS, #PAC 74-104.328, EDWARD REINIG PHOTO

IRON FRONT HOTEL

The Iron Front Hotel was built in 1889 on property known as the Aught Claim in Last Chance Gulch. House Republican members of the first Montana State Legislature regularly convened in the fourth-floor meeting rooms.

The facade is made up of pre-formed cast iron sections which were assembled on the site. The locally mined iron ore was cast at the Jonathan Stedman Foundary only two blocks away. Of notable interest are the wide fluted pilasters extending from the ground to the cornice and the upper floor windows which are separated by short iron columns and have semi-circular arches with elongated keystones. The building is a recipient of commendations by the Friends of Cast Iron Architecture of New York City and is the only building of this type in Montana and possibly the only such building between the West Coast and the Mississippi River.

The building was originally known as the Windsor House and later as the Odd Fellows Hall and the Templeton Hotel. It has also served multiple functions with commercial space on the ground floor, hotel apartments on the second and third floors, and a meeting hall/vaulted ballroom complex on the top floor. The storefront space was first occupied by the Helena Hardward Company until about 1910.

Jared and Laura Bert purchased the building on the 400 block of Main in August 2003. They inherited over 100 years of history, including the ghost that has been rumored to roam the fourth floor Windsor Ballroom. The ballroom is the focal point of the old hotel which still offers 35 rooms and apartments for rent. The dance floor was once rated as the best in the west and is built upon springs for a softer touch to the dancers' feet. The Berts have restored the ballroom which has a 30-foot ceiling and is surrounded by a balcony on three sides.

The Windsor House, which gave its name to the ballroom, was a popular rest stop for travelers to Helena arriving at the railroad depot, and just three blocks west of the Iron Front.

The Iron Front is worth a stop on a trip to Helena, not only to see the building but to shop in the specialty stores on the first floor. The Berts can be reached at (406) 442-4889.

The elaborate Iron Front Hotel in the early 1900s. MHS, #953-201

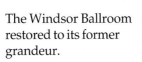

The Windsor Ballroom restored to its former grandeur.

PLACER HOTEL

One of Helena's largest downtown historic buildings was, for over 60 years, the social and political center of the city. In the 1880s, several small shops occupied a site at the southeast corner of Main and Grand streets on Last Chance Gulch. The Thompson Block was built on the site in 1888. It housed the Northern Pacific Railway office as well as clothing, tailoring, hat, gun and furniture shops.

In 1911, local businessmen invested in a new hotel project to be the largest and most splendid in town. Helena's most prolific early 20th century architect was hired to design the hotel. The total cost for construction was about $450,000 plus $11,000 for furnishings. Rumors had it that placer gold found in the gravels removed for construction helped pay some of the bills. On April 12, 1913, the grand hotel opened. In its heyday, the hotel was favored by the state's lawmakers when they were in town, and lobbyists for powerful state interests often entertained there. It was also known for its elegant dining and reception rooms, and became the center for hosting many social events.

The seven-story brown brick building is an imposing structure on the Gulch. Built on sloping ground, a series of shops faces Last Chance Gulch on the first floor, while at the rear, ground level is at the second floor, facing Jackson Street. The design is symmetrical with a central, recessed entry on the front and brick piers with sandstone caps that support the building and separate the storefronts. The building's parapet features wide eaves with decorative braces above an ornate cornice.

In 1961, Prudential Diversified Services took over management and named the hotel The New Hotel Placer. But through the years the Placer met the same fate as most older, downtown hotels being not modern enough and the profusion of large motel chains in the area. The hotel closed and was converted to apartments and retail space with Last Chance Gulch reverting to a pedestrian mall. However, the exterior of the Placer has lost none of its early 1900s elegance.

The proud old hotel is an anchor building on the Last Chance Gulch pedestrian mall in downtown Helena.

FROM
PLACER HOTEL
HELENA, MONT.

To_____

_____

_____

THE GATES OF THE MOUNTAINS,
ONE OF HELENA'S SCENIC FEATURES

The Placer Hotel under construction, Dec. 9, 1912. MHS, #953-553

Montana Daily Record, April 5, 1913.

PLACER HOTEL TO OPEN TODAY NOON

INFORMAL RECEPTION WILL BE HELD AND ORDERS SERVED AT THE CAFE.

The Placer hotel will be opened for business at noon today. An informal reception will be held this afternoon and evening, excellent music will be provided and the cafe will be prepared to serve orders to guests. Every person in the city is invited to examine the new hostelry from the basement to the seventh story. The banquet room, the grand saloon, the ball room and in fact the entire building will be open to inspection.

One week from today the state ball and banquet will be held at the new hotel, when it will be formally opened to the public. Preparations for not more than 250 persons are being made by the management. Reservations for tables, carrying with them admission to the ball, must be received not later than April 11.

About 150 persons have made reservations already, and of this number half are Helena people. The other half are residents of Butte, Great Falls, Missoula, Billings and others of the larger towns throughout the state.

HOTEL PLACER

EUROPEAN PLAN

HELENA, MONT.

Opens at Noon Saturday, April 5, 1913

MODERN AND FIRE PROOF.
HOT AND COLD WATER IN EVERY ROOM.

IN THE CENTER OF THE BUSINESS DISTRICT

ALL STREET CARS PASS THE DOOR.
RATES: FROM $1.50 A DAY UP.

State Ball and Banquet Saturday Eve, April 12

TABLES MUST BE RESERVED BY APRIL 11.
MAURICE WEISS, MANAGER.

Montana Daily Record, April 4, 1913.

MODERN EUROPEAN PLAN
SPECIALLY LARGE SAMPLE ROOMS

HOTEL PLACER

HELENA'S NEW FIRE PROOF HOTEL
RATES $1.50 UPWARD

MAURICE S. WEISS
MANAGER

HELENA, MONTANA.

PLACER HOTEL

THE GATES OF THE MOUNTAINS.
ONE OF HELENA'S SCENIC FEATURES.

HELENA, MONT.

A 1914 postcard view of the lobby from the mezzanine.

A 1916 postcard view of the hotel.

A 1957 postcard view of the hotel.

The Cheerio Cocktail Lounge was located in the hotel for many years. This menu is from 1942 and apparently has messages from sweethearts to the boys going into the service.

HOTEL ALBERT

The Hotel Albert, a four-bedroom bed and breakfast, is one of only a few structures in the little hamlet of DeBorgia, in the westernmost section of Mineral County, just off I-90. The building's construction in 1911 was part of the rebuilding of DeBorgia after the great forest fire of 1910 which burned down the town along with three million acres of forest.

Edward Albert, who owned a sawmill in the area, used his own lumber to build the hotel to serve the rail passengers who came through town on both the Northern Pacific and Milwaukee railroads. A saloon was built next to it. Emma Albert ran the hotel, which was first named Hotel DeTousia, while Edward ran the saloon. The hotel originally had six rooms, an outhouse and outdoor shower.

Mr. Albert died in the 1950s and his wife in 1967 so the hotel sat abandoned until the late 1970s or early '80s when a succession of owners worked on restoration and tried to run it as a paying business. In 1993, Pam Motta from Missoula purchased the building, fixed it up and ran it as a four-room bed and breakfast. It had a cozy early 1900s atmosphere set in the isolated area of western Mineral County. The original red cedar floors, wood trim and wainscotting remain intact, along with 10-1/2 foot high ceilings. The bed and breakfast has been closed for over a year now but Pam Motta still resides in the building.

Rumor has it that Charlie Chaplin was in Butte when he was notified by wire of his screen test in Hollywood. Traveling by rail, he stopped in DeBorgia and reportedly stayed in the room at the front of the hotel, up the wooden spiral staircase from the registration desk. There is also the doctor's room at the top of the stairs, so named because a visiting physician reportedly used the room to treat patients because of the natural light provided by the three tall windows.

The Hotel Albert was apparently first named Hotel DeTousia and was built in 1911 after the disastrous forest fires of 1910 which destroyed DeBorgia.
MINERAL COUNTY HISTORICAL SOCIETY

HOTEL DEER LODGE

At the corner of Main and Missouri in Deer Lodge, Powell County, is one of the largest buildings in the downtown area.

On April 12, 1911, the *Silver Star Post* reported that Leopold Schmidt "has great faith in Deer Lodge and its future and is willing and already making arrangements to invest considerable money in its enterprises and to start new ones." Schmidt had managed breweries in Deer Lodge and Butte, and served in the Montana Legislature. He had gone to Washington in 1896 and founded the Olympia Brewing Company. In 1911, he was back in Deer Lodge to promote a new hotel.

In late April 1911, the Deer Lodge Hotel Co. was incorporated for $75,000. Schmidt was the heaviest individual investor. The three-story brick building with 52 guest rooms and 14 offices on the east side of the second floor opened on March 20, 1912. Mayor Frank Corley and his wife were the first guests.

Deer Lodge citizens were proud of their new

hotel and it was called "one of the finest in Montana" because of its elevator and hot and cold running water in all the rooms. The hotel remained open for business until Sept. 30, 1986, when it closed for good. The building was used for retail purposes for years and as a Senior Citizens Center but has been boarded up for several years with no indication of a new use.

The hotel Deer Lodge in 1915.

Two views of the old hotel as it looks today.

HOTEL MEADE

On July 28, 1862, the discovery of gold in Grasshopper Creek brought the first major rush of gold seekers to this remote area of southwestern Montana in what would become Beaverhead County. The town of Bannack (a misspelling of the Bannock Indians) had a population of 3,000 by the next year and was the new territory of Montana's first capital. After the gold was depleted in a few years, the capital was moved to Virginia City in 1865 and the county seat to Dillon in 1881. By the 1940s the town was nearly deserted. The town was designated a state park in 1954 and a National Historic Landmark in 1962.

Bannack was designated the county seat of the newly formed Beaverhead County in the Territory of Idaho in 1863. A two-story brick building was erected in 1876 to serve as the county courthouse. It was built in a modified Greek Revival-style, with some aspects back to the Federal period. Its original dimensions were 33 feet by 60 feet.

The Nez Perce War of 1877 brought Chief Joseph and his band to the edge of town. The courthouse, being the major masonry building in town, was fortified to serve as both a military headquarters and a refuge for women and children. The approach of General O.O. Howard's troops prevented the Indians from attacking the town.

When the county seat was moved to Dillon in 1881, the building was remodeled into a hotel, named The Meade. An ''L''-shaped addition was constructed to the rear of the building and a front porch built. The building has an attic, a basement crawl space and a large curved staircase leaading to the second floor, with oak flooring in the main first floor room. Several vaults from when the building was a courthouse are still in place.

With the demise of the town through the years, the buildings of Bannack were neglected and abandoned. Today, while the building is still the most prominent in town, it shows its years of wear and tear from both people and the elements. Now only a couple of ovens and a sink remain as testament to the hotel's former elegance. Floorboards and staircases creak. Gaps in the masonry allow sunlight to stream through parts of the building and graffiti is evident on the plastered walls which show signs of peeling off the underlaying lath.

LARRY ROLAND PHOTO

Labor Day celebration in front of the hotel on Sept. 7, 1925.
BEAVERHEAD COUNTY MUSEUM ARCHIVES 406.1C-8(2)

The Hotel Meade as it looked in 1934. The lattice railing on the top of the porch has been removed by this time and the town had only a few residents. GALLATIN COUNTY HISTORICAL SOCIETY, P6505, 95.568

HUNTER'S HOT SPRINGS RESORT

There is hardly any trace of one of the state's largest and most popular resorts of the late 1800s and early 1900s, Hunter's Hot Springs Resort near Springdale in Park County and 20 miles east of Livingston. The springs were discovered in 1864 by Dr. Andrew Jackson Hunter. He was with one of the first wagon trains coming into Montana over the Bozeman Trail and was hunting a few miles north of the Yellowstone River. Hunter was familiar with similar mineral waters of Hot Springs, Arkansas, and he staked a claim to the site before proceeding on with the wagon train.

In 1870, Hunter returned to the upper Yellowstone Valley and built a house near the springs. He also built a dam between the hot and cold springs and made a pool which was used by both the whites and the Indians of the area. Three years later, he built bathhouses and began to develop a sanatorium. In 1878 a post office was established and in 1882, the Northern Pacific came through the valley opening up an easy access to the growing resort. A year later a hotel with full facilities was opened. Hunter's son-in-law, Frank Rich, built a second hotel, known as the lower house, to provide for guest overflow.

The Montana Hot Springs Company from Bozeman purchased the fledgling resort in 1885, built a 40-room hotel, and in 1886, platted a townsite. The town to be known as Mendenhall was named for one of the principals, Cyrus Mendenhall. While the town never really developed, the resort continued to flourish.

A brochure for the resort claimed the waters had curative powers for diseases of the digestive, nervous, uterine and urinary systems, diseases of the skin and other unclassified diseases. It even stated that, "combined with modern medicine...syphilis, acquired and inherited, responds more promptly to radical and permanent cure than to any other system or place of treatment known to the civilized world."

In 1898, the resort was bought by Mr. James A. Murray, a millionaire banker from Butte, who would be involved in other hotel projects in the state. He

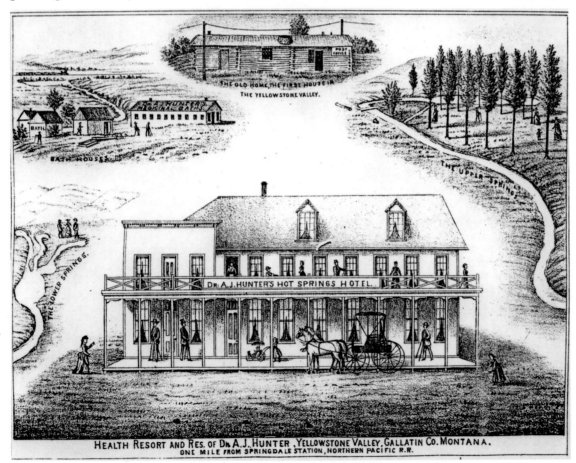

The first hotel constructed by Dr. A.J. Hunter.
GALLATIN PIONEER MUSEUM #P1653

-154-

installed a bottling plant at the site and built a second section of the hotel, known as the Upper House, with 100 rooms heated by hot water from the springs. The resort quickly became a popular destination with excellent cuisine and service. Carriages met the trains at nearby Springdale and brought the guests to the hotel.

The conversion of the resort into one of major proportions occurred in 1909 when Murray commissioned the construction of a grand hotel which he named the Hotel Dakota. The solid concrete building was two stories in height with a 450-foot frontage and a depth varying from 100 to 250 feet. More than 250 guests could be housed at any one time. It was a Mission-style with a wide two-story veranda more than 400 feet long, located to take advantage of the dramatic view. The pool section was reached by an enclosed corridor; the pool itself was 103 feet by 50 feet with 40 dressing rooms on each side. On the east end of the building was the solarium, a semi-circular glass structure 50 feet across. Murray had invested more than $150,000 in the grand hotel.

Rates were $1.00 a day for a room, $1.50 a day for a room with hot and cold running water, and $2.00 a day for a room with running water and a toilet. A herd of milk cows supplied milk and cream, fresh vegetables came from the gardens and a farm provided broilers and eggs. The grounds had a golf course, tennis courts, and riding horses. Hunting and fishing were available. Several small kiosks or gazebos were scattered across the grounds with spigots so that guests could sit and drink the supposedly curable waters in the shade.

The resort was boasted in brochures as the most complete hostelry west of St. Paul. But this would not last for long. When the automobile became popular and roads improved it was expected to increase business, but it had a different effect. Travelers tended to travel farther and spend less time in a given place. In 1916, prohibition was enacted in Montana and the resort had a well-stocked supply of wine and liquors to serve its guests. Determined to continue the supply regardless of the law, the management set up a distillery in a tree-shaded hollow and made fine bourbon which they bottled at their old plant and sold to guests.

On Aug. 1, 1914, a caravan of 250 automobiles left Minneapolis and traveled over a proposed highway for a direct route to Yellowstone Park. Their destination was Hunter's Hot Springs and the new highway would be named the Yellowstone Trail. Unfortunately, the new highway bypassed the resort and fewer and fewer cars turned off to the resort.

With bootlegging the reputation of the resort deteriorated and in the 1920s, it was no longer considered a family place. A disastrous fire on Nov. 3, 1932, finally ended the illustrious career of Hunter's Hot Springs/Hotel Dakota. A fire in the old frame part of the building started during remodeling and quickly consumed the entire structure.

The plunge survived the fire and was shortly reopened. A Quonset hut was placed over the pool and it continued to operate as a pool until it closed in 1974. Thus Hunter's joined several other large mineral/hot springs resorts that fell victim to fire and the changing modes of transportation and life styles. Today there are hardly any remnants of the resort to see.

A panoramic view of the majestic Hotel Dakota.
YELLOWSTONE GATEWAY MUSEUM OF PARK COUNTY

A pre-1909 view of the resort. GALLATIN COUNTY HISTORICAL SOCIETY, #P2392N

The back side of the hotel and plunge in 1910. GALLATIN COUNTY HISTORICAL SOCIETY, #P2390N

Interior of the Natatorium or Plunge. GALLATIN COUNTY HISTORICAL SOCIETY, #P2391N

Guests on the veranda of the Hotel Dakota that stretched the length of the building. GALLATIN COUNTY HISTORICAL SOCIETY, #P6995N

The Lower Spring, Hunters Hot Springs, Montana.

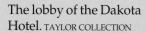

The lobby of the Dakota Hotel. TAYLOR COLLECTION

The Lobby, Dakota Hotel, Hunters Hot Springs, Montana.

The solarium in the Hotel Dakota was stocked with ferns, palms and other greenery and had easy chairs, couches and deck-type chairs for rest and relaxation. TAYLOR COLLECTION

The Solarium, Dakota Hotel, Hunters Hot Springs, Montana.

The New Dakota Hotel,
Hunters Hot Springs, Montana.

TAYLOR COLLECTION

HUNTER'S HOT SPRINGS

NORTHERN PACIFIC
RAILWAY

IN THE ROCKIES OF MONTANA

Hunter's Hot Springs, Montana, Dec. 9, 1906

Hunter's Hot Springs
Montana

KALISPELL HOTELS

NORDEN HOTEL

The Norden Hotel, known as the Bjorneby Building and the Silver Block, was built in 1903 as a lodging house. The two-story building is located at 24 - 1st Avenue West in Kalispell. The building served as Kalispell's only hospital from 1905-1909 and from 1909 to about 1955 was known as the Hotel Norden. It was managed for many years by the Frederick Brothers.

These Norwegian brothers hired Norwegians to work in their hotel and dining room; the business catered to the working class and to county residents who came to Kalispell to do business in the county seat. The hotel was vacant in 1928 but opened again in 1930. In the early years, one could get a family-style dinner at the hotel for 25 to 35 cents. Rooms were $1 per night, as compared to $2 at some of the other hotels in town.

From 1912 to 1944, the building was owned by real estate agents Griffin & Stannard and then an heir of Griffin's. From 1955 to 1976, the hotel was called the Frontier Hotel. Today it is the Rosebrier Inn, an assisted living center.

The Montana Hotel at 142 First Avenue, on the corner of Second Street and First Avenue in the 1920s. MHS, #94-774

The Montana Hotel was built between 1907-09 and was a hotel until about 1975. At one time there was the Buffalo Cafe and dance hall in the building. In 1984, it was converted to office space.

Karst's Ranch

This resort, located on U.S. Highway 191, 35 miles south of Bozeman in Beaverhead County and 56 miles north of West Yellowstone, was one of the first resort ranches, or dude ranches in the state of Montana.

Pete Karst, a native of Wisconsin, came to the Gallatin Valley in the late 1890s, working as a freight hauler. He homesteaded a property that he would later build into a world famous resort. He constructed a log building and a bunk house, and in 1907, the first guests arrived from the Midwest for a hunting and fishing vacation.

First called "Karst's Cold Springs Resort," the dude ranch grew to become a favorite western retreat. In 1905, Pete began to build cabins, eventually he had 25 spaced along the bank of the Gallatin River. By the 1920s the resort, now known as "Karst's Ranch," had electricity, accommodations for 150 guests, a dining room, bar, dance hall, store, gas station, museum, swimming pool, stable and even a ski jump, built across the river which attracted world-class ski jumpers in 1937.

Karst also ran his Karst's Stage Line up and down the Gallatin Valley for many years. He was also known as the "Asbestos King" as he discovered the mineral in the mountains behind the resort. He turned his resort over to two men from Billings in 1953 and on Jan. 25, 1957, a fire completely destroyed all the main buildings (he had eventually built 40 cabins along the river). The resort was rebuilt twice but in the 1970s, fire again destroyed the buildings, and today nothing remains of this well-known old resort. Pete Karst died in 1966 at age 89.

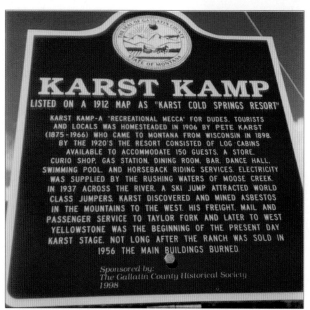

A late 1940s brochure for the ranch.

Interior of the resort's main lodge. GALLATIN COUNTY HISTORICAL SOCIETY, 90.2597, P1833N, B.H. ALEXANDER PHOTO

The resort in the 1940s. GALLATIN COUNTY HISTORICAL SOCIETY, 90.2636, P1873N, B.H. ALEXANDER PHOTO

The cabin line along the Gallatin River in the 1940s.

Kootenai Lodge

In years previous to the advent of white settlement in the Flathead country of Northwest Montana, the site of Kootenai Lodge on Swan Lake in Flathead County was visited frequently and occupied at least seasonally by Flathead, Kalispell and other Indian Nations native to the Northwest.

Kootenai Lodge, the country "camp" of Cornelius Kelley and Orvis Evans, is perhaps the most finely crafted and elegantly appointed collection of "rustic" log buildings in the state. Set in a remote part of mountainous northwestern Montana and constructed at a cost of no less than $2 million, Kootenai Lodge represents a most unusual juxtaposition of urban opulence and Arts and Crafts-inspired rustic architectural design. Kelley and Evans were aspiring young lawyers for the Anaconda Copper Mining Company when they together purchased the site of Kootenai Lodge on Swan Lake in 1908. By 1911, Kelley had risen to the vice-presidency of ACM and Evans became chief counsel for both ACM and the Montana Power Company. When Kelley was named president of ACM in 1918, he and his family moved from Butte to an 80-room Georgian mansion near Manhasset, New York. Evans had been offered a vice-presidency at this time but he chose not to leave Montana.

For the first few summers at Kootenai Lodge, the Kelley and Evans families lived in the small, original log cabins and shared a single log building for cooking and dining. The 1920s signalled a major construction boom at the lodge. Originally conceived to be a quiet summer retreat for the Kelley and Evans families, Kootenai Lodge, when completed, became a luxurious country resort, a place to entertain the business associates and corporate executives of the Anaconda Copper Mining and Montana Power companies, many of whom travelled to Montana for the summer months from the East Coast.

The resort was apparently another hangout for western artist Charlie Russell. He painted there and throughout the entire landscape of huge lawns and rock flower gardens were sketches of wildlife and Indians done in cement. Huge parties were given and guests were taken on boat trips and saddle horses were provided for riding. Besides Russell, prominent guests included Will Rogers, John McCormick, Dixie Lee, later to become Mrs. Bing Crosby, and Queen Wilhelmina of the Netherlands, who was a principal stockholder in the Anaconda Copper Company

The families traveled to the property by private railroad car to Whitefish and then took chauffered

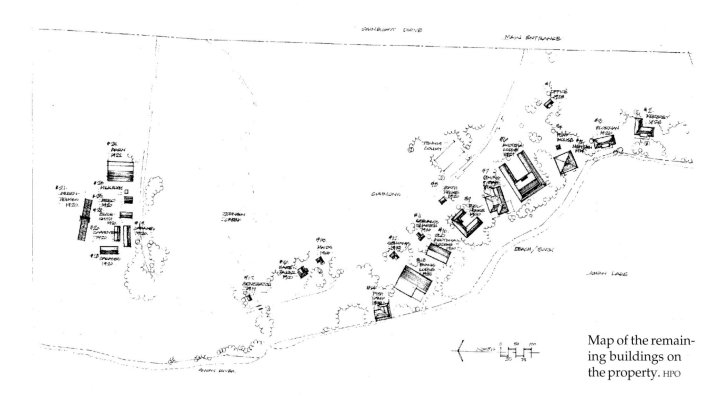

Map of the remaining buildings on the property. HPO

limosines which were ferried across the Swan River on log rafts. In 1931, Lewis Evans and Cornelius Kelley became the sole owners. Kelley died in 1957 and, in 1968, his heirs sold the 2,400-acre resort to the Stoltze Land and Lumber Company of Columbia Falls for $600,000. Timber was harvested and part of the land was subdivided into building lots.

Forty-two acres, including the historic buildings, were later sold to Mr. and Mrs. Sig Brekkeflat of Bigfork. A group of investors bought the resort in 1982 for $1.25 million and turned it into a private membership club. They have spent considerable money upgrading the 23 historic buildings, including two large lodges, the Kootenai (1921); the Evans (1925); Pool House (1900); Dining Room and bar (1915); 31-stall horse barn (1922); officers, servants quarters, service buildings and guest cabins. Included is 2,600 feet of Swan Lake and Swan River frontage.

Two views of the 1921 Kootenai Lodge, which is 70' x 50' with six bedrooms, fireplaces, a ballroom, an elaborate dining room, a butler's pantry and a game room. All the furniture was made out of local wood, the floors were polished hardwood and the cooking was done on wood stoves even after the resort was wired for electricity. HPO

 # LENNOX HOTEL

The Lennox Hotel/Wold's Agricultural Implements Building at 219-221 West Main Street in Laurel, Yellowstone County, is associated with the second phase of commercial development in the town following a disastrous 1907 downtown fire. The 1908 building replaced a wood-frame structure dating to the early 1900s and was the first to incorporate brick into its construction. The two-story building had a one-story brick addition added to the rear sometime in 1934. When the building was completed, the bottom floor contained commercial space and the upper floor had 32 guest rooms. Also in 1934, the building was sold to Ole M. Wold and the hotel was converted into the Lennox Apartments. In 1944, substantial changes had been made to the exterior facade and the upper floor was converted to commercial use. The ground floor had many uses including a grocery store, a hardware store, a dry goods company, a furniture store and a car/truck dealership.

MACQUEEN HOUSE

The MacQueen House in Miles City, Custer County, was built in 1882 by William N. MacQueen, who arrived in the cattle town in 1880 to represent commercial interests from St. Louis. He built the finest hotel in this part of eastern Montana in 1882 and called it the Inter Ocean Hotel. MacQueen later became the post trader at Fort Keogh, a major U.S. Army post in Miles City. In 1885, the name was changed to the MacQueen Hotel and had 86 rooms, steam heat, electric bell in each room, red velvet carpet in the halls and most rooms, folding beds, marble-topped dressers, commodes and arc lights. In the parlor were huge gilded, framed mirrors that reached from the ceiling to the floor; there was a wide veranda along the north and east side of the first and second floors. In 1897, the hotel met its end when it burned down.

The MacQueen House in the 1880s.
MHS, #981-541, L.A.
HUFFMAN PHOTO

MISSOULA HOTELS

issoula had an abundance of hotels through the years, being on the mainline of the Northern Pacific Railroad and a major commerce center for western Montana. It is also the oldest large city in the state with a mill built at the confluence of Rattlesnake Creek and the Clark Fork River in the mid 1860s. Of all the dozens of hotels built in the past 140 years, 10 former hotel buildings still exist in the downtown area. Today the Doubletree Hotel and Holiday Inn offer rooms and convention facilities in the downtown area.

LENOX HOTEL

The Lenox Hotel building at the corner of Woody Street and West Broadway was built between 1902 and 1911. It became a hotel in 1915 and in later years served as the county's pre-release center and office space. In recent years, homeWORD restored the building and converted it to apartments and office space.

BELMONT/VICTORIA HOTELS

The Belmont Hotel, on the left, in the 400 block of North Higgins was built between 1902 and 1911. It served as a hotel from 1911 to 1940 and has now been restored to apartments with retail space on the ground floor. The Victoria, right, was built in the same time frame. It continued to serve as a hotel into the 1950s and is retail space.

BRUNSWICK HOTEL

This old hotel building is at the corner of Railroad and Woody streets near the railroad tracks. It is a two-story triangular-shaped building erected between 1890-91. It is one of the oldest remaining hotel buildings in the downtown area. Associated with Missoula's first railroad building boom, it was part of a once-thriving commercial district running along Woody Street, south of the old NP depot. It was converted into apartments about 1930 and has had various commercial tenants since then.

Atlantic Hotel

The three-story Atlantic Hotel at 519-23 North Higgins Avenue was constructed in 1902. In the early days it contained a hotel, restaurant, saloon and barber shop. Prominent Missoula architect A.J. Gibson designed the building. Today a secondhand store occupies the first floor.

Montana Hotel

The Montana Hotel was built by John Maloy in 1887. He served as proprietor until 1891 when Otto Siegel purchased the business. The hotel building is on West Railroad Street. It catered to passengers arriving on the Northern Pacific Railroad. In 1948, Walter Staves opened The Electric Shop in the building. It is probably the oldest building in the downtown area and is a significant historical structure that now houses an antique mall. CHUCK HURT PHOTO

Northern Hotel

A.J. Gibson designed the Northern Hotel at 201 West Railroad sometime between 1902-1912. It was known as the Norden Hotel from 1917 to 1930 with George Briggs as the proprietor. In 1932, it again became the Northern Hotel. In 1974 it opened as The Depot Restaurant.

Missoula Hotel

One of the most imposing old buildings in the downtown area is the Missoula Hotel at the corner of Main and Ryman streets. The building was built in 1891 and is closely linked with the early railroad era. It served as the center of operations for the construction of the Coeur d'Alene branch of the Northern Pacific Railroad in 1891. William Kennedy and Samuel Mitchell built the hotel, and Kennedy, who also owned the Rodgers Hotel, was elected Missoula's mayor in 1891. The building was known as the Missoula Hotel until about 1932 when it became known as the Missoula Hotel and Apartments. The original hotel had a bar and billiards parlor, an arcade joining the front and rear sections, a laundry and two dining rooms in the rear section. The middle section of the building which included the arcade was filled in in 1926. For years the basement of the hotel contained the Cafe Montmartre and Jungle Club but today the building has a clock repair shop and apartments. The facade has changed considerably through the years as can be seen from the photographs.

A 1916 view of the hotel before the Ryman Street facade was filled in.

Compare the facade changes in these two photos. Above 1940s, below, present day.

HOTEL MISSOULA — MISSOULA, MONTANA

CAFE MONTMARTRE — Cocktail Lounge in Connection

MENU

MISSOULA HOTEL
CAFE
MONTMARTRE
and
JUNGLE CLUB
MISSOULA, MONTANA

PALACE HOTEL

The Palace Hotel was originally built as the Savoy Hotel in 1909 and changed to the Palace in 1911. It is located at the corner of Broadway and Ryman streets. There were 125 rooms and suites with baths, telephones, running water, steam heat, electric lighting and an elevator when it opened in 1909. In 1941, an annex was built to the east thus expanding it to the biggest hotel in downtown Missoula. The five-story (original and annex) hotel was forced to close in 1980 due to economic conditions. Today it has a restaurant, bar and lobby on the first floor and remodeled apartments on the next four floors.

A 1923 view of the hotel before the annex was added to the east.

The hotel after the 1941 addition to the east.

A 1911 view of the hotel's lobby. FRANK HOUDE COLLECTION

New Year Dinner, 1914

RELISHES

Celery, 30c   Olives, 25c   India Relish, 25c   Young Onions, 15c

OYSTERS

Blue Points on Half Shell, 35c   Olympia Oyster Cocktail, 35c
Blue Point Cocktail, 35c   Special Select Raw, 35c

SOUPS

Cream of Tomato, 10c   Chicken Broth, en Tasse, 15c

FISH

Fried Filet of Flounder, a la Colbert, 45c
Baked Lake Superior Trout, Duglaree, 45c
Fresh Cracked Crab with Mayonnaise Dressing, 60c
Special Little Neck Clams, Steamed, and Drawn Butter, 35c

ENTREES

Chicken Hash in Cream with Mushrooms, 50c
Breaded Veal Chops and Green Peas, 50c
Fried Chicken Livers on Toast, 60c
Club Steak a la Palace, 55c

ROASTS

Roast Prime Ribs of Beef, 50c; Extra Cut, 80c
Roast Young Duck, Apple Sauce, 60c
Stuffed Jumbo Squab, on Toast, 50c
Roast Suckling Pig, Sage Dressing, 60c

VEGETABLES

Red Cabbage, 10c   Brussel Sprouts, 20c   French Peas in Cream, 20c
Au Gratin Potatoes, 15c   French Fried Sweet Potatoes, 20c
Baked or Mashed

SALADS

Sliced Tomatoes, 30c   Cucumbers, 30c   California Head Lettuce, 30c
Chicken Salad, 45c   Crab Meat Salad, 30c   Lobster Salad, 30c

DESSERTS

Apple Pie, 10c   Hot Mince Pie, 10c   Pumpkin Pie, 10c
English Plum Pudding, Hard or Brandy Sauce, 15c
Chocolate Eclairs, 15c   Sponge Cake, 10c   Fruit Cake, 10c
Ice Cream and Cake, 15c   Raisins and Nuts, 15c

CHEESE

Camembert Cheese, 25c   Roquefort Cheese, 25c   Pimentos Cheese, 25c
Toasted Bents Water Crackers, 10c
Coffee, Tea or Milk.

Try our Special Palace Cocktail 25c

A 1914 New Year's dinner menu.

The hotel today is still one of the largest buildings in downtown Missoula. It has been converted to apartments with retail businesses on the ground floor.

FLORENCE HOTEL

A n 1895 view of the first Florence Hotel. The band of the 25th Infantry from Fort Missoula is in front of the building. This building burned down in 1913. UM #84-305

The second hotel on the site was built in 1913 and burned down in 1936. Construction on the third hotel building started in 1940.

The Florence Hotel was the hub for Missoula's business and social life from the time it opened in 1941 until it closed its doors in 1976. Out of the ashes of the second hotel building, was formed the Missoula Real Estate Association. Its president was

Walter McLeod; vice president was state Senator John L. Campbell; secretary-treasurer was L.E. Bunge and on the board were H.O. Bell, W.L. Murphy, Walter Pope, James Caras, Sid Howard and William Steinbrenner. The new $600,000 building, designed by G.A. Pehrson of Spokane and built by Spokane constructor Alloway & Georg, would have seven stories, 175 rooms, a main dining room, coffee shop, cocktail, lounge, banquet rooms and several retail outlets. With the advent of Missoula's growth away from the downtown area and many national chains moving into town, it was no longer economical to keep the hotel open and it was closed and essentially turned into office space with a new name–the Glacier Building. Today it is called The Florence and is owned by the ALPS Corporation. Its outside appearance reminds one of its past splendor and importance to the city. This view if from the 1950s.

Coffee Shop - New Florence Hotel
Missoula - McKay -

The elegant lobby area from the 1940s has been restored to its original look by the ALPS, Corporation.

Menu cover.

A modern view of The Florence building at the corner of West Front Street and Higgins Avenue.

GRAND PACIFIC/KENNEDY/
PARK HOTEL

The building was built on Circle Square at the end of Higgins Avenue in 1903. It was opposite the busy Northern Pacific Depot. It was first called the Grand Pacific Hotel but by 1913, it's name was changed to the Kennedy Hotel. The fountain in the center of the photo was built in 1913 with large pieces of native stone brought in from the surrounding mountains. It was put there as part of a plan to create an aesthetically pleasing northern entrance to the city from the railroad depot.

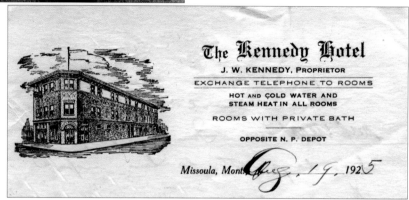

The Kennedy Hotel

J. W. KENNEDY, PROPRIETOR

EXCHANGE TELEPHONE TO ROOMS

HOT AND COLD WATER AND
STEAM HEAT IN ALL ROOMS

ROOMS WITH PRIVATE BATH

OPPOSITE N. P. DEPOT

Missoula, Mont. Aug. 19, 1925

By the time this post card was sent in 1931 the name had changed to the Park Hotel. For years the hotel was a bar on the main floor and has now been converted to the Park Place Apartments.

ELECTRIC LIGHTS, TELEPHONES, HOT AND COLD WATER, STEAM HEAT

GRAND PACIFIC
HOTEL

(EUROPEAN PLAN)
CHAS. A. SCHRAGE, Proprietor

The Most Conveniently Located Hotel
IN MISSOULA

OPPOSITE NORTHERN PACIFIC STATION   MISSOULA, MONTANA

1913 ad.

The Hotel Paxson building at the corner of Ryman Street and West Broadway. It was built between 1902 and 1912. The second and third floors served as a hotel, the bottom floor was a garage. Today an import market and bar occupy the ground floor.

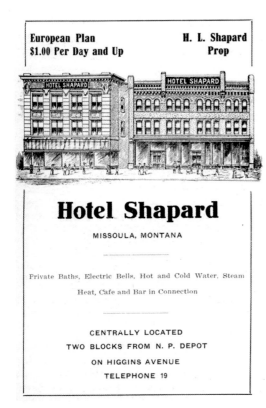

European Plan $1.00 Per Day and Up

H. L. Shapard Prop

Hotel Shapard

MISSOULA, MONTANA

Private Baths, Electric Bells, Hot and Cold Water, Steam Heat, Cafe and Bar in Connection

CENTRALLY LOCATED
TWO BLOCKS FROM N. P. DEPOT
ON HIGGINS AVENUE
TELEPHONE 19

1910 ad.

E. LACASSE   J. LACASSE   A. J. SPOONER

ELECTRIC LIGHTS   STEAM HEAT

EUROPEAN PLAN

Windsor Hotel

SPOONER-LACASSE CO., Propr.

E. LACASSE, Manager

DINING ROOM IN CONNECTION

MISSOULA, - - - MONTANA

1913 ad.

HOTEL MARGARET

The elegant Hotel Margaret was located on the Big Blackfoot Milling Company property in Bonner, just east of Missoula. It was built in 1892 and named for Margaret Robinson, one of Bonner's first school teachers. It provided accommodations for visitors and employees of the mill. Its interior was decorated with elegant carvings done by craftsmen from the mill. The townsite of Bonner was named for prominent businessman E.L. Bonner and the first mill was constructed there in 1886. The hotel was razed in March 1957 with some of the interior furnishings and woodwork given to the University of Montana.

The lobby of the Margaret with the ornate woodwork. JACK DEMMONS COLLECTION

The Margaret was the center of social activity for the lumber community of Bonner, seven miles east of Missoula. The Big Blackfoot Milling Company is in the background. JACK DEMMONS COLLECTION

Montana (Marcus Daly) Hotel

Surely one of Montana's most ornate and beautiful hotel buildings when it was constructed in 1888, stands today as a mere shadow of its illustrious past. Situated at the corner of Park Street and South Main in Anaconda, the county seat of Deer Lodge County, its history is intertwined with Marcus Daly, of the famed Copper Kings of Montana Territory and the fight for the siting of the permanent capital city.

In April 1888 a group of prominent Anaconda citizens met to discuss their city and decided what it needed was a good hotel in hopes this would help entice the capital of the new state of Montana to move there. One of the men, Marcus Daly, said, "Go ahead with your plan and find out what has to be done, and put me down for one-half the investment."

Thus a hotel association was formed with Daly as president. The plans for a three-story brick hotel were prepared by W.J. Boyington, an architect from Chicago, Illinois. His plan called for a 120-foot-square structure, three stories high. It would be built of brick with rich ornamental work in terra cotta. Originally to cost $90,000, an additional $15,000 was included for a mansard roof. However, it was suggested after the hotel construction had reached its intended three stories to add an additional floor instead of the mansard roof to improve the hotel's appearance.

In early 1889, the hotel was at the point where furnishings were being ordered and D.L. Harbaugh of St. Paul, Minnesota, formerly with the Palace Hotel in San Francisco, was hired as manager.

On June 27, 1889, the *Anaconda Weekly Review* stated, "Next Monday, July 1, 1889, the finest and best-equipped hotel in this part of the country with all modern improvements will be open to the public of this city, and in fact to the public of the Territory. Fifteen hundred invitations have been issued to people here and in all parts of the union. The ball in the evening will surpass for excellence of dress anything of the kind ever attempted in Montana. Special trains will come into Anaconda during the day from Helena, Butte, Deer Lodge, Dillon, Great Falls, and in fact every city of town of any importance in the Territory." A gay affair it certainly was, for the following week some two columns of newsprint space was given over to a vivid description of the attire of the ladies in attendance.

The newspaper went on to describe the layout of the hotel, "The main floor will abound with cozy nooks where millionaire and miner may chat, where the lounger will find quiet retreat, and where half Montana's politicians may meet at one time and not

Only the bottom two floors remain of this once majestic building.

seriously jostle one another."

The final cost was $135,000 and shortly after Daly died in 1900 it was remodeled at a cost of $96,000. Daly had high hopes for the hotel and should Anaconda be selected as the new state's capital, it would house the legislators. Unfortunately, Helena was selected as the new capital city and the hotel was often nearly empty.

For a long period of time the hotel was owned by the Anaconda Copper Mining Company. They sold the structure in October 1954 to the Edmiston and Bell Company of Kalispell, who operated the hotel for a short time and then decided to demolish the structure. A local citizen's group was formed to save the historic hotel. The group purchased the building in 1964, and made plans for renovation, plus the addition of a motel to be attached to the southeast corner of the building by a breezeway. The 125 rooms, 80 of which had the original fireplaces, were brought up to date and the name was changed to the Marcus Daly Hotel to honor the man who had so much to do with its initial establishment.

Unfortunately with the mining and smelting business in the area on the decline, the owners of the hotel could not continue to operate it. It was decided to demolish the top two floors in the 1970s and turn the first two into retail and office space. The building is now a mere shell of what it was and Montana lost one of its grandest structures.

An 1888 architect's drawing of the Montana Hotel.

The ornate back bar was molded after the Hoffman House bar in New York City. It filled the south wall of the hotel's bar, the Tammany Lounge, and was built of mahogany complete with massive, hand-carved columns and large mirrors. When part of the hotel was demolished in the 1970s, the bar was bought by bid and moved to Seattle. MHS, #957-285

"Tammany" was one of Marcus Daly's thorough-bred race horses and proved himself one of the greatest winners of all times. In a match race with an Eastern horse named "Lamplighter" and a bet of $40,000, "Tammany" won easily. Daly was credited with winning a quarter million dollars on this race. It took the bookies two weeks to pay the bets he had won. In memory of this famous horse, Daly commissioned a New York artist to do a life-sized head shot of "Tammany" on the bar room floor. The head was designed by Tiffany and Sons in New York City, carved from colored hardwoods and inlaid on the floor. This masterpiece of nine square feet cost approximately $3,000. The lounge in the hotel is named "Tammany Lounge." MHS, #957-286

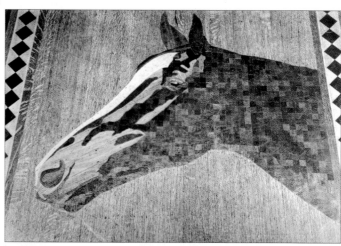

A 1911 postcard view of the hotel.

An early 1900s view of the hotel. MHS, #940-396

PHILIPSBURG HOTELS

The Kaiser House was built by Michael Kaiser, founder of the Philipsburg Water Company, in 1881. It is one of the town's oldest existing masonry structures. The original hotel boasted a wrap-around porch extending halfway around the building. Second-story French doors, matching windows below and four Norman arched double doors with fan transoms display its excellent design. The hotel had a bar and billiard room and a large dance hall on the second floor. At one time the building was connected by a roof walkway with the Stevens Hotel just behind it, and housed a fraternal organization known as The Redmen. The building has also housed a doctor's office and a stained-glass shop. It is now under restoration. The building sits at the upper end of Main Street in Philipsburg, Granite County.

A band playing outside the Pintler Hotel in the 1920s.
GRANITE COUNTY HISTORICAL SOCIETY

GRANITE COUNTY HISTORICAL SOCIETY

The Courtney (Pintler) Hotel was built in 1918 by Morris and Humphrey Courtney with profits they made in mining in the area during World War One. The basement housed the Granite County garage, the first floor the Overland Car dealership and the top two floors, a hotel and offices. Many of the rooms were occupied by area school teachers. The Courtney brothers owned the hotel building until the 1950s when it was sold to the Immenschuh family who continued to operate it as a hotel, bar and restaurant for many years. In 1990, the family gifted the building to the Granite County Museum and Cultural Center which operates it today. This is one of the attractions in this small mining community in Granite County which has seen an insurgence of historic rehabilitation in the last few years.

PIPESTONE HOT SPRINGS

Until its closing in 1963, Pipestone Hot Springs in Jefferson County was one of the oldest and longest-running hot springs resorts in the state. A late 1880s issue of *The Holiday Inter Mountain* gives a capsule history of the site at that time:

"Twenty miles southeast of Butte, in a beautiful valley of the Rocky Mountain main range, is located the popular health resort and watering place known as the Pipestone Springs. Legal title to the land was first acquired in 1868 by a party of prospectors who were attracted by its sheltered position and other natural advantages for winter habitation. Mr. John Paul, an honest and enterprising old-timer, bought the property in 1870, and began ranching there, as the surrounding country affords the finest winter range in Montana, on account of the light snowfall and abundant grasses. Mr. Paul established his residence in the valley at a point two miles from the base of the mountains and close to the thermal springs which have since become so famous for the health-giving properties of their waters. In 1878 extra buildings were erected for public accommodations, and the place became locally celebrated as a health resort, Mr. Paul having leased it to other parties. Some wonderful cures were effected, and many invalids suffering from rheumatism, neuralgia, dyspepsia, paralysis, kidney and liver complaints, impure blood, lead-poisoning, etc., experienced speedy and permanent relief after a course of bathing and drinking. The water has a natural temperature of 106 to 146 degrees Fahrenheit, and is strongly impregnated with iron, sulphur, soda, magnesia and other minerals. During the past season Mr. Fred A. Stuart has had charge of the springs, and the accommodations have been greatly enlarged and perfected, a new hotel having been built with all the conveniences and improvements necessary to insure the comfort of ladies and children, as well as members of the sterner sex. In short, there is no place in Montana where health and pleasure can be more successfully courted, or where the surroundings are more cheerful. Connected with the springs, and owned also by Mr. Paul, is a tract of fine hay land, containing 400 acres, a fine orchard five acres in extent and a large area devoted to the cultivation of vegetables and small fruits. It is certain that in the near future Pipestone Springs will enjoy a reputation as a health resort second to none

on the Pacific coast, for it is the intention of the management to add yearly to the already great attractions of the place, and to keep prominently before the public the facts concerning the wonderfully curative properties of the waters. The Springs is connected with Butte by a tri-weekly stage service, affording easy and pleasant communication."

John Alley, an attorney for the Anaconda Copper Company, bought the resort in 1912. This was a great place for Butte and other area residents to go for relaxation in the years before World War One. Two railroad mainlines came close to the resort, stagecoaches and, eventually, automobiles provided access. A 25- by 100-foot indoor pool, "The Plunge," 100 canvas-roofed guest cabins, vapor and hot mud bathing facilities and a hotel constituted the area. The hotel burned down in 1913 and a second one was destroyed by fire in 1918.

An insert in the July 22, 1918, issue of the *Montana News* of Butte had an article concerning a prominent Butte businessman and the resort:

"It was King Canute who commanded the waves to stand back from Albion's stores, and Joshua, the sword arm of the Lord, who ordered the sun not go down until the slaughter of the enemy hosts of Israel should be completed; Mahomet directed the mountain to come to him. These constitute the outstanding orderings of several men of achievement. Now comes Jim Finlen of Butte who would do a thing that may dim the luster of the reputations of these ancients. He would pluck from the land of the lotus a full-fledged bathing beach and plant it mid-mountain in Montana for the joy of the joyous. He has not done this as yet, but the betting is odds-on that he will, because in Butte they call him Finlen the Finisher, which is another way of saying that what he starts he completes.

"Where mountain and plain meet, on the eastern slopes of the Continental Divide, just over the hills from Butte, is a dimple on nature's face. All about it are rolling foothills, green carpeted. And in the heart of a vale through which a gurgling brook threads its way, is the right spot, Pipestone Springs. This is the stage setting of nature for the camouflage of the sea which Finlen and his landscape gardeners and architects propose to paint.

"Finlen is the head of a syndicate, which has acquired the Pipestone property. He proposes to make of it, through the expenditure of several thou-

Today the enclosed pool hut and the old guest lodge are still standing on one side of the hot springs road.

On the other side of the gravel road to the west are the remains of an old dance pavilion and a gazebo over one of the springs.

Southeast of the pool and guest lodge are 19 remaining guest cabins barely visible in the large cottonwoods.

sand dollars, the greatest of inland watering places. The syndicate will build a great hotel, a hospital over which physicians who understand the curative properties of the springs will preside; baths, in which the Pipestone waters will wash away rheumatic twinges and make ancient kidneys new, and cause old Ponce de Leon, if still in communication with what is doing on earth, to regret that he did not wait several hundred years and come to the right place for the restoration of his youth. There will be golf links for the golfers, and trout ponds for those who would angle, together with all the attractions that are found at a sea shore resort. Everything that man can devise to fit in with nature's lavish endowment of Pipestone, will be done and when it is all completed it will be the mecca of the ailing and the playground of all the west.

"But the big feature of the undertaking will be an artificial beach, which will describe a graceful curve of several hundred feet in length immediately facing the broad veranda of the hotel that is to be. The bottom and shelving sides of the beach will be cemented for cleanliness but it will have the ocular effect of a sea shore bathing place. It will be fed by living springs of hot water, constantly changing, and from the veranda guests may sit in comfort and watch the water nymphs disport themselves in the inland sea that Jimmie Finlen has brought to Montana for them. Perhaps their bathing suits will be short as the breath of men whose girth is great from years of full feeding, and fit as though the nymphs had been melted in all their loveliness and poured into them. If so, speed the day of the hotel's completion.

"Over the hills from Butte winds one of the most beautiful mountain automobile roads in the Rocky mountains, and the distance can be covered on high in 40 minutes. Both the Milwaukee and the Northern Pacific railroads pass close to the springs, so it is comfortably close to the great center of population of Montana.

"It is not probable that the work of building the hotel will be undertaken until after the war, and the present structure, a small but comfortable tavern, will be made to do until that time. But the other improvements, aside from the hotel, will be made as soon as possible, and much of the work should be completed early next season.

"The waters of Pipestone are famous. Their virtues are such that federal experts long ago recommended the purchase of the property by the federal government.

"It is a big undertaking. Can Finlen do it? Just

watch his smoke. He has made a reputation and a fortune in his management of a Butte hotel, which before he took charge of it, had a private financial graveyard of its own. And he has associated with him a group of men who can help, including Roy S. Alley, John Corrette and Ray Rhule, and others, all individuals who occupy places of vantage in Butte's business life."

Sometime after 1918 a small, nine guest room hotel building, with a lobby and dining room was built near the pool, which was covered by a Quonset hut. Business steadily declined through the years until 1963 when the hotel was closed to the public.

Remains of some of the buildings can still be seen just off Delmoe Lake Road, off exit 241 on Interstate 90.

1887 ad.

"The Plunge" at Pipestone Hot Springs. The once outdoor pool apparently was covered at one time by a large wooden building, but is now enclosed by a large quonset hut. Date unknown.
GALLATIN COUNTY HISTORICAL SOCIETY

An early postcard view of the resort. TAYLOR COLLECTION

The City of Polson began in the late 1870s and was incorporated in 1910. The opening of the Flathead Reservation to settlers in 1910 brought many people to Polson. It is believed the Lake Hotel was built around 1909 to accommodate the influx of people. The hotel played an important part in the trade and commerce of the area and shipping on the lake itself. The hotel was considered "The Hotel" by residents and people traveling up and down the lake and retained its importance as a resort hotel until the Salish House was built a few years later.

The Lake Hotel building was a two-story, parapeted frame building of unequal U-shape plan. The facade was altered through the years to give a much plainer look than the original construction. It was razed in 1984 and, in 1999, a dentist's office was built on the site.

The old Salish House building at the northwest corner of Main Street and Second Avenue (U.S. Highway 93) is one of the most prominent buildings in downtown Polson. The structure is a three-story, irregular shaped, brick constructed building which looks out upon Flathead Lake to the north and the Flathead River to the west. The building has essentially four sections: the three-story main structure that fronts both Main Street and Highway 93; the three-story wing that projects at an angle from the main building and fronts on Main Street; the one-story restaurant addition that is attached to the north wall of the wing; and the two-story wing which was built on the west of the original section along Highway 93.

The hotel has been a community landmark since its construction by Frank Swanberg of Missoula. Construction of the $75,000 hotel on the site of the old Grandview Hotel started in the summer of 1927.

The Lake Hotel. HPO

The grand opening was in June 1928 with ex-governor Joe Dixon as the main speaker and Jimmie Harbert presiding over the banquet and ceremonies. The facility had a 150-seat dining room; 26 rooms, 12 with baths; steam heat and hot and cold water in every room. One of the first tenants was the J.C. Penney Store which moved into the building in May 1928. The name of the hotel was selected from 362 contest entries.

Harbert, a prominent Polson businessman took over management of the hotel and for the next 44 years, the hotel had a succession of owners and managers. In 1976, the hotel became the first Polson business to adopt a nautical look and assume nautical names for its various divisions–Lighthouse Inn, Ancient Mariner Restaurant, Blackbeard's Cove Lounge and Popeye's Bar. Finally, in 1986, the Whitefish Credit Union acquired the property in a sheriff's sale.

The building has had a number of businesses in it through the years and even provided a stage for the Port Polson Players. In 1993, long after the building ceased to be a hotel, a restaurant, bar and casino opened for business.

RAVALLI HOTEL

Hamilton's largest hotel was built for the town's founder, Marcus Daly. He first visited the Bitterroot Valley in 1864 and later made his fortune in the copper mines of Butte. He returned in 1887 to purchase large tracts of land for his Bitter Root Stock Farm and to harvest timber for his mines in Butte. The town was named for James Hamilton, a Daly employee, who platted it in 1890. By 1900, when Daly died, the town was the county seat of Ravalli County and the commercial center for the Bitterroot Valley.

Daly built his Ravalli Hotel in 1895 at the corner of Second and Bedford directly across the street from the county courthouse. He built the hotel, in the Colonial Revival-style for $35,000, to handle the overflow from his house for all his friends and business associates who came to visit him. The hotel was a large, three-story brick veneer building with a lobby, dining room, billiard and bar room on the first floor. Fifty guests rooms were on the top two floors. A structure at 212 South 3rd (now the Bibler Apartments) served as the laundry room and servants' quarters.

He had extensive landscaping done around the hotel and had a wooden sidewalk built to the fairgrounds, east of town, which was used as a horse riding path. In 1919, the hotel burned and only the servants' quarters and laundry room survived. The bricks, which came from a kiln just west of Hamilton, were reused in a building at 213 West Main in the downtown area. The hotel site is now occupied by the Bedford Building (Hamilton City Hall).

Group of touring visitors at the hotel, circa 1907. TOP: MHS #948-097, BOTTOM: #948-098

-185-

Suggestions for Breakfast

RAVALLI HOTEL, HAMILTON, MONT.

1909 postcard view.

AN ORDER to the Dining Room can be telephoned from any room by simply giving the number of the breakfast wanted and time same is to be served.

SERVED IN MAIN DINING ROOM ONLY from 7:00 A.M. until 10:00 A.M. Sundays 8:00 to 10:30 A. M.

An extra charge of 25c will be made if served in room

No Substitution Allowed

CEREALS

Oatmeal with Cream	15c
Wheat Flakes	15c
Cornmeal Mush	20c
Cream of Wheat	20c
Puffed Rice	15c
Force	15c
Maple Flakes	15c
Grape Nuts	15c
Shredded Wheat Biscuits with Cream	15c
Corn Flakes	15c

CAKES, ETC.

Buckwheat with Maple Syrup	15c
Buckwheat with Honey	20c
Wheat with Maple Syrup	15c
Wheat with Honey	20c
Fried Mush with Maple Syrup	20c
Fried Mush with Honey	25c

TOAST

Dry Toast	10c
Buttered Toast	10c
Dipped	10c
Milk	20c
Cream	25c
French Toast	25c

Stevensville Hotels

Stevensville, in Ravalli County, is considered to be the oldest established community in the state (circa 1830s). In the early 1900s it grew due to the establishment of orchards in the area. Six miles north of town on the benches along the Eastside Highway was a 30,000 acre orchard development with plans for a new town, called Bitter Root. A hotel, known as the Bitterroot Inn, was built at the end of Sunnyside Ridge, constructed of logs and designed by famed architect, Frank Lloyd Wright early in his career. The building was com-pleted in 1910 and orchards were planted in the area in 1910-11. The Big Ditch Company, which lent its carpenters to build the inn, moved their office and employees into the building in 1911.

A small post office was established in the inn, for the town which never went beyond the planning stage. On July 28, 1924, the inn caught fire and burned to the ground. Later a barn was built on the site but it too burned down. Several other homes attributed to Wright are still in existence in the upper Bitterroot Valley.

Bitter Root Inn, Stevensville, Mont.

Stevensville Hotel, STEVENSVILLE, Mont.

Located at the northwest corner of Second and Main streets. The Whaley brothers owned the hotel, dining room and bar. Fire started in the hotel's attic on Oct. 7, 1919, and burned almost half of the business part of town. Hardly anyone was in town because everyone was at the Ravalli County Fair in Hamilton for Stevensville Day. UM, #76-52

SUPERIOR HOTEL

The Superior Hotel in Superior, Mineral County, was a two-story wood structure built in 1892. It gained its place in history as the first hotel that Gideon bibles were placed in. In the early 1900s, three Gideon bible salesmen gathered in a hotel in Janesville, Wisconsin, discussing the possibility of placing bibles in hotel rooms. The suggestion went to a Gideon cabinet meeting in 1907 and the plan was adopted in 1908. Twenty-five bibles were ordered for the Superior Hotel apparently because they thought the town was wide open and would need the word of the Diety. The Milwaukee Railroad was pushing through the area at the time and workers were coming in from all over the world. The name of the hotel was later changed to the Ordean Hotel and the building was destroyed by fire in 1940.

An early 1900s view of the hotel. MINERAL COUNTY HISTORICAL SOCIETY

One of the largest commercial buildings along Main Street in Thompson Falls was, at one time, one of the largest and finest hotel facilities in northwestern Montana. It was opened in 1908 and named after Edward Donlan, the eldest son of Edward Donlan.

The elder Donlan was very important to the development of Thompson Falls. He was born in Quebec and at the age of 12 left home and went to work. He ended up in Neihart, south of Great Falls, and by 1895 he owned his own sawmill. His political career started in 1892 when he was elected as a Republican state senator from Missoula County (Thompson Falls was in Missoula County at that time). He was elected again in 1906, 1910 and 1918. He ran unsuccessfully for governor in 1908 even though he had the backing of the powerful Anaconda Copper Company.

In the early 1900s, he expanded his lumber operations and had extensive land holdings in Thompson Falls as well as east and west of town. He founded the Thompson Falls Mercantile Company and was instrumental in getting the town named the county seat of the new Sanders County. He was also a key figure in getting the Thompson Falls Power Company to construct a dam adjacent to the town, which proved to be a major factor in the growth of the town.

The original design for the hotel included 30 rooms, an office, bar, restaurant and a full basement for a power plant and laundry room. Furniture was brought from Chicago and the hotel opened on May 24, 1908. In 1911, a back kitchen was added and the restaurant was expanded. Donlan also built a two-story brick annex which increased the hotel capacity to 50 rooms. A 1928 fire destroyed most of the annex and the second floor also had to be removed.

James Rhoades, the mayor of Missoula, bought the hotel business along with John Scott in 1913. Rhoades soon sold out to Scott and there followed a series of owners through the years. Donlan sold the building in 1915. In the 1930s, the name was changed to the Black Bear Hotel and in the 1970s to the Townhouse Hotel. The hotel was the social center of town until its closure years ago.

Donlan left Thompson Falls in 1913 and moved to Milltown, near Missoula. He eventually lost his fortune and died in 1952. Today the hotel sits fondly waiting for its next career.

SANDERS COUNTY HISTORICAL SOCIETY

WARM SPRINGS RESORT

erhaps the most unusual resort in Montana's history was the Warm Springs Resort in Deerlodge County. The resort is now the site of the Warm Springs State Hospital, just off Interstate 90. It was also one of the oldest resorts as Louis Belanger built the first bathhouse there in 1865.

Six years later, Belanger and his brother-in-law, Elisha Gerard, built a two-story hotel and summer bathhouse. Their new resort became well-known for its cuisine and its dancing parties. In 1877, the resort changed hands and mission.

Dr. Charles F. Mussigbrod and Dr. A. Mitchell received a contract from the Territorial government to care for residents who were declared "insane." They were paid a dollar a day for each patient. They built an additional two-story hotel for guests at the resort, which consisted of 12 rooms and two parlors. An additional two-story house was built for convalescent patients and another house for more violent patients. Three plunge baths were built nearby, one each for male and female patients, and one for resort guests. Thirteen "insane" patients were admitted when the facility opened in April 1877.

With both an asylum and a resort co-existing in the same place, no incidents between the people were reported. The most prominent feature of the facility was, and still remains, the "deer lodge" mound. This 40-foot high carbonate mound is about 30 feet in diameter. The springs that issue water from its top is 172 degrees Fahrenheit, one of the hottest geothermal springs in Montana. Other hot springs bubbled from the base of the mound, all with a high iron content in the water.

An observation deck was erected on the mound in 1878 and remains today. An article in the 1885 *Rocky Mountain Husbandman* stated: "Water rises so that it may be reached with a dipper, but we believe it does not flow over. It is the favorite spring for drinking. From the summit of this mound one has a fine view of the splendid valley. At the foot of the mound numerous small springs burst out, and it is from there that the baths are supplied."

The resort and asylum seemed to work out together but by 1912, when the state legislature purchased the asylum, the resort had already closed. The asylum was renamed the Warm Springs State Hospital and at its peak in the 1950s had 2,000 patients. It has now been downsized considerably with patients being placed back into community facilities. The only remains of the old resort is the large mound on the far side of the state hospital grounds. One can still drive to the mound but not climb on it. No building remains are in evidence today.

Two views of the massive hot springs mound and observation building on top. All that remains of the popular resort from over 100 years ago.

WELLS HOTEL

Garnet in Granite County is one of the best-preserved and most popular ghost town destinations in the state. It is located in the Garnet Range in Missoula County, 11 miles off Highway 200 and 10 miles off Interstate 90 near Bearmouth. The area is administered by a cooperative agreement between the Bureau of Land Management and the Garnet Preservation Association.

Mining in Garnet began in the late 1800s and continued into the 1930s. During the boom years, the population reached several thousand. A hotel, store, Chinese laundry, school, several saloons, drug store, assay office, barber shop and private cabins for the miners and their families were constructed. The buildings were put up quickly and without foundations, which contributed to eventual collapse.

Mr. and Mrs. J.K. Wells came to Garnet from Beartown sometime before 1898. Prior to living in Garnet, they had built and been proprietors of a hotel in Beartown. When they arrived in Garnet, Mrs. Wells began designing another hotel, modeling and fashioning it off one in Beartown. The hotel opened on March 17, 1898, with a festive celebration. People came from neighboring towns such as Missoula, Deer Lodge and Butte. Upon completion, it became the largest building in Garnet. After the hotel closed in the 1930s, Frank Davey, who owned a general store in town, moved into the kitchen and lived there until his death in 1947.

The hotel, now open to the public for viewing, is a two-and-one-half-story wood frame building with a steeply pitched gable roof. Its dimensions are 50 feet by 30 feet. A wooden walkway was located in front of the building, but it is gone now. The first floor had five rooms: a parlor, an office, a dining area, a kitchen and a pantry. The second floor contained eight rooms. Some sort of pulley system was devised on the front entrance of the second floor in order to bring trunks to the second floor. Before weather and vandals took their toll, one would have entered through beautifully carved doors with stained glass windows. To the left was the ladies parlor, on the right stood the hotel office, and moving forward the guest would enter the grand dining room. Such events as the Grande Masquerade, the Hard Times Ball, and the St. Patrick's Day Calico Ball were held in this room.

Although this was a very modern building, there were no plaster walls or insulation. The walls were covered by cloth-backed paper. Heating the large building required two stoves in the dining room. Upstairs rooms were heated by rising warm air. Access to these rooms was by an oak staircase. Miners who could not afford a private room would rent floor space on the third floor. Lines on the floor divided it into spaces for the men to lay out their bedrolls under the sky lights.

The outhouse was behind the hotel and could be reached by descending a few steps from the second floor. The interior of the lower regions was heavily whitewashed for the ultimate in sanitary conditions.

After the Wells Hotel closed in the '30s, Frank Davey moved into the kitchen. Davey maintained several rooms for visiting friends, but in unkept rooms mushrooms grew out of the still-made beds. When Davey died in 1947, everything left in the hotel was sold at auction.

The hotel has been stabilized through the years and is a good example of a modest hotel that served the citizens of a remote early mining town.

LARRY ROLAND PHOTO.

The Ritchey Hotel was another large hotel in Garnet. It was built in 1898 by Henry Schoenfeldt and was named for Samuel Ritchey who discovered the rich, red ore of the Nancy Hanks mine. That discovery, in 1896, led to the founding of Garnet. The hotel was located a short distance from downtown Garnet and burned down in the early 1900s. GARNET PRESERVATION ASSOCIATION PHOTO

An early view of Garnet with the Wells Hotel on the extreme right. Davey's Store is in the middle.

WOLF CREEK HOTEL

In 1886-87 the Montana Central Railroad wound its way through the steep Prickly Pear Canyon, an area prized for its superb trout fishing. The town of Wolf Creek, named after an Indian word meaning "Creek That the Wolf Jumped In," grew to serve the railroad from Carterville, which was a mile farther west.

James Carter built a small one-story hotel here in 1887. He soon sold the hotel to a young Englishman, Charles Forman, who replaced it with a three-story frame building circa 1892. Forman attached his new hotel to the original manager's house, covering its log walls with clapboard siding. Its simple no frills style was once a common sight across rural Montana.

Ten rooms and home-cooked meals offered respite for outdoor enthusiasts, stage and railroad travelers. Forman, a butcher by trade, also operated a livery stable and meat company. The small house out back, once filled with ice from the Missouri River, kept his larder cool. The hotel operated from 1887 to 1984 under only five owners. It served as a stage stop on the Mullan Trail and routes from Helena to Augusta and Fort Benton. Later it sheltered workers who built Holter Dam in 1910, and gas pipeline laborers in the 1930s.

The Forman family sold the hotel in 1927 for $12,000 to Leo and Pearle Leedy Rhein, who sold it in 1946 to Robert and Gertrude Funk. In 1964, John and Dorothy Floberg purchased the hotel. They rented the rooms at $5.00 a night and sometimes rented then twice each day for one or two dollars, as workers on the new Interstate highway crews changed shifts.

Although now under the shadow of the interstate, its time-layered walls earlier witnessed high winds and waters, fires, births and deaths. Since 1994, Rick and Helen Greenlee have owned the old hotel and have restored it as a private home.

The Best Western Jordan Inn and Convention Center in downtown Glendive, Dawson County has been a fixture in town since 1901. It was built by Mr. & Mrs. William F. Jordan and originally had 150 rooms. At one time there was a bowling alley in the basement and a funeral home also operated out of the basement. In 1972 an addition was completed with an indoor swimming pool and sauna. A priceless art collection of Montana artist J. Kenneth Ralston is displayed in the hotel along with a collection of agate jewelry. There is a casino, the Range Lounge and a full dining facility to accommodate the many tourists that pass through the area in the summer and also the local trade. In addition to 82 Best Western class rooms, the hotel also has some mini-apartments that are rented by the month. #223 North Merrill, Glendive, MT 59330, Phone 1-800-824-5067

The Howdy Hotel in Forsyth, Rosebud County will have its 100th anniversary in 1905, still run by the fourth generation of the same family. Originally called the Hotel Commercial and built when the railroad came through town, the name was changed to the Howdy Hotel in 1950 and the interior changed to a western decor in the 1950s. In the early days, the hotel was in competition with the other hotel in town that catered to the cowboy trade. Today the hotel has 30 apartments, which can be rented out by the night or long-term and 10 rooms. There is also a bar, 24-hour cafe, antique shop and barber shop. The hotel has never closed in its 100-year history. 807 Main Street, Forsyth, MT 59327, phone 1-888-23-HOWDY

HOLLAND LAKE LODGE — POSTAL ADDRESS: SEELEY LAKE, MONTANA

The first hotel on Holland Lake, in the northern part of Missoula County off Highway 83, was the White Hotel built in 1918. It burned down in 1950 and was replaced by the present Holland Lake Lodge, which is still a popular resort on the lake.

The Park Hotel Block in Livingston, Park County, on the corner of West Callender and Second Street was built in three stages between 1910-1917. The original hotel was built at the corner of North Second and Park Street, now the Masonic Building. The Park Hotel Block now houses retail outlets on the ground floor.

The Rainbow Hotel building on Main Street in Shelby, Toole County, is waiting for someone to resurrect it.

The Hotel Valier in Valier, Pondera County was completed in 1908. It was a rather large hotel for such a small town.

The Lalonde Hotel in Sidney, Richland County billed itself as the "Pride of Eastern Montana" with 80 rooms, all with baths, a coffee shop, dining room and cocktail lounge, and a banquet room with seating up to 200.

The Hotel Shannon in Glasgow, Valley County.

Nine Mile, 30 miles west of Missoula, became a regular stage stop in the 1870s when gold was discovered near Martina, a settlement located 20 miles up the Nine Mile Valley. George H. Brown built this two-story hotel, restaurant and dancehall in 1893 at the lower end of the valley. The Nine mile House was operated by Brown until his death in 1912. His son, George A. "Nine Mile" Brown, then operated the business until the late '30s. Several owners operated the hotel until Ralph Chapel purchased the business and built the present Nine Mile House across the road in 1946-47. Today it is a popular bar and restaurant.

The Milligan Hotel in Miles City.

Sleeping Child Hot Springs Resort, southeast of Hamilton, Ravalli County, was a popular resort for many years but has been closed to the public for some time.

BIBLIOGRAPHY

Birkby, Jeff, *Touring Montana and Wyoming Hot Springs*, Falcon Publishing, Helena, 1999.

Burk, Mary K. with Bruce T. Burk, *Dusty Trails Up Lolo Creek, The Don Babcock Collection, A Pictorial Journey Through the Heart of the Bitterroot Mountains*, Laughing Stock Press, Lolo, 2002.

Everett, George, *Champagne in a Tin Cup, Uptown Butte and the Stories Behind the Facades*. Outback Ventures, Butte, 1995.

Moylan, Bridget, *Glacier's Grandest, A Pictorial History of the Hotels and Chalets of Glacier National Park*. Pictorial Histories Publishing, Co., Inc., Missoula, 1995.

State Historic Preservation Office & Montana Historical Society–National Register of Historic Places through 2000, Helena.

Additional information was gathered from the Montana Historical Society Library, the State Historic Preservation Office files, various newspapers and magazines, and the files of many statewide museums and libraries.

ABOUT THE AUTHOR

Stan Cohen is a native of West Virginia and a 1961 graduate of West Virginia University with a degree in Geology. He has been a resident of Missoula since 1961 and has been a consulting geologist, engaged in the ski business and has been involved in various museums through the years. He established Pictorial Histories Publishing Co., Inc. in 1976 and has authored or co-authored 73 books and published over 300. He has published Montana books on World War II in the state, a history of Region One of the U.S. Forest Service, the 1910 forest fire, the forest fires of 1988, a history of smokejumping, histories of Fort Benton, aviation history in the state, the University of Montana and many books on Missoula's history. He lives with his wife, Anne in a 1909 Queen Anne home in Missoula.

For a catalog of Pictorial books:
Write to: Pictorial Histories Publ Co. Inc., 713 South Third West, Missoula, MT 59801
or
See our website–www.pictorialhistoriespublishing.com